DIGGING DEEP, AIMING HIGH

DIGGING DEEP, AIMING HIGH

An Educator's Lifelong Quest to Put Kids First

STEVEN ASKINAZI

Paperback ISBN: 978-1-64718-995-2
Hardcover ISBN: 978-1-64718-996-9
Epub ISBN: 978-1-64718-997-6
Mobi ISBN: 978-1-64718-998-3

Published by BookLocker.com, Inc., St. Petersburg, Florida.

Printed on acid-free paper.

BookLocker.com, Inc.
2021

First Edition

Editor: David Aretha

To protect the privacy of individuals who are still living, some names and details have been changed. The following is the author's personal recollection of the events of his life and career.

Library of Congress Cataloguing in Publication Data
Askinazi, Steven
Digging Deep, Aiming High: An Educator's Lifelong Quest to Put Kids First by Steven Askinazi
Library of Congress Control Number: 2020918137

To my wife, Helene, who continued to put her own needs and career aspirations second to the well- being and love for her family. Without her daily support and understanding I could not have devoted so much time to my own endeavors. Her inspiration and assistance in helping me to get this book off the ground have led me to this place in time.

Contents

About the Author

Steven Askinazi had a long and successful career association with the New York City public schools and the City University of New York. As a student attending Public School 75 in the Bronx, Campbell Junior High School, and John Bowne High School in Queens, he knew early on that teaching was going to be his chosen career. After receiving a BA and MS in Education, with a minor in Spanish language at Queens College, Steve became permanently certified to teach in grades seven through twelve. Having spent a year studying and living in Spain under the sponsorship of the City University of New York Study Abroad Program, his newly acquired linguistic skills prepared him for a career working in the South Bronx and East Harlem. His entire work experience was invested in two heavily populated Spanish-speaking environments, which always made him feel at home. After teaching for twelve years in middle school as a teacher of Spanish and Bilingual studies, he received a transfer to The Manhattan Center High School for Science and Mathematics.

Having completed a second master's degree in Supervision and Administration from Hofstra University, Steve became certified as an assistant principal. He served as a teacher of Spanish and English As A Second Language (ESL) at Manhattan Center while taking on the additional position of supervisor of Humanities at the school. Twelve years later he became the principal of the school, overseeing the River East Elementary School, Isaac Newton Junior High School, and Manhattan Center High School, which were all housed in the same building. Steve also worked as an ESL instructor in the evenings at Rockland Community College for several years.

After retirement, Steve became a consultant for the National Academy Foundation, serving as a mentor to principals in the Miami public high schools. He worked with the foundation for seven years.

Steve is married to a former teacher who is also a product of the NYC public schools and the City University system. He has two daughters living in New York, one who teaches Special Education in Queens and one who is the director of Global Alumni Relations for a law firm.

As a family, we have never forgotten our roots and continue to give back to communities of underserved populations.

Preface

The decision to share my story was a difficult one and a long time in the making. Over the years, my storytelling of educational experiences with colleagues, friends, and family, who were so far removed from the New York City school experience, was met with mixed reactions. Some were intrigued, others were skeptical, and still others were totally indifferent.

The impetus to convey my experiences was a combination of encouragement by my wife and daughters and the realization that sixteen years after my retirement, I am still passionate about the profession that I chose so many years ago. I also take personal pride in the successes I achieved, which I document in the chapters that follow. In addition, I would like to bring awareness to the fact that fifty years after my initiation into the New York City public school system, so little has changed, in spite of demonstrated solutions to the struggles that prevent us from doing better. In many educational systems we continue to fail to replicate best practices or model programs that work.

Pockets of talent are present in every part of the country, with numerous Blue Ribbon and Magnet schools providing deserving kids with a stellar education. Yet, nationwide, many school districts continue to be segregated and the chasm between the "haves" and the "have nots" has widened exponentially.

Teacher education programs continue to fail to better train candidates for a very difficult and challenging job. Performance expectations for educators as well as for students are a far cry from what should be required and, yes, demanded. Sadly, the decisions as to how to educate our children come down to a power struggle between municipal and district governments, school boards, unions, politicians, and community leaders, with the interests of the children rarely being taken into account. We continue to fight City Hall for basic necessities. In many schools we often see revolving doors where poorly prepared teachers leave after a couple of years to enter other industries. The lack of support, mentorship, and direction contribute to educators becoming demoralized and feeling helpless. While this disappointment for our workers might be common early on in other career areas, the time and money lost in education while we are trying to get this right causes irreparable harm to our children. The contents of this book will address these issues and demonstrate how one very special school was able to overcome these problems in a successful and productive way.

I was accompanied on this forty-year journey by four teams of individuals who held me up, pushed me forward, and celebrated my accomplishments.

The first team consisted of my family. My wife and I were raised in the Bronx, attended NYC public schools, and continued our studies at Queens College of the City University of New York to earn our professional degrees. Public education was ingrained in our being. Yet, the world in which I was teaching was incredibly different from the one in which we were living. Residing in a middle-class suburban area, our own children were unaccustomed to seeing apartment buildings, burned-out storefronts, homelessness, and poverty. Nevertheless, they eagerly participated in my school activities. My family chaperoned school trips, attended school functions, and partied with the kids. This experience holds fond memories for them and helped sensitize them to the plight of those less fortunate. We all decided as a family that we would give back to the very same communities that helped us become educators.

The second team consisted of the players in the trenches. I owe a great deal of gratitude to the teachers, administrators, paraprofessionals, aides, office staff, and security personnel who worked in concert to create miracles in an extremely adverse environment. They are my heroes. Their perseverance was unrelenting. Their firm belief that "failure was not an option" and their risk-taking in thinking out of the box, sometimes circumventing established rules, created an atmosphere where the children truly became their number one priority. These folks are the true outliers in society.

The third team was made up of my advocates in the field; those who fought hard for my appointment to Manhattan Center, first as a teacher, then as an assistant principal, and finally as principal. For each person who fought for me, there were five who fought to prevent my promotions. Whether it was a function of union regulations, Department of Education seniority rules, licensing requirements, or the world of Civil Service, there were those who tried to block my future in the field of education. Nevertheless, I owe so much to John and Stephanie Ferrandino, who believed in me from day one. John headed up the High School Division and endorsed my placement as principal. Stephanie, a principal herself, was a mentor to me and to so many others because of her dedication to the profession and her deep understanding of what constitutes great leadership.

Lastly, but importantly, I thank my team of thousands of students and parents who welcomed me into their world, knowing full well that I wasn't from their *hood*. I am eternally grateful to them for trusting me, for embracing me, and for bringing me into their families.

I wrote this book as a primer on what can be accomplished when you put kids first, when you bring together a team of supporters who envelop the students with hope and love, and when you create a culture that aims high. With these ingredients, you can make miracles happen.

Steven Askinazi
December 2020

Chapter 1 – In the Beginning

The year was 1968, a year filled with turmoil, both domestically and worldwide. It was also a year that changed the soul of education in New York City.

The war in Vietnam was sucking up thousands of our citizen workers on a daily basis, depositing these poorly prepared fighters into the swamps and jungles of a third world nation. Each evening, the number of American soldiers killed in the war would stream across the bottom of everyone's television screen. It was depressing for all of us; frightening for prospective draftees and their families.

Canada became a safe haven for those who chose to avoid military service by renouncing their U.S. citizenship in exchange for their lives. Thousands of corporate men as well as students in disciplines other than education left the confines of their comfortable offices and classrooms to take positions in the New York City Public Schools and acquire a 2S draft exemption. Others joined the National Guard, believing it was a safer alternative to involuntary conscription. Regulations regarding teaching exemptions as well as student exemptions nationwide were confusing and inconsistent. However, in New York

City, it seemed to be a well-received idea. Hundreds of men who cared less about teaching and devoting a career to teaching underprivileged inner-city kids took positions away from those who had put in four to six years of study in order to enter the teaching profession.

Racial tensions were bringing out the worst in people. Martin Luther King Jr. and former President John F. Kennedy's brother, Senator Robert Kennedy, were all murdered within months of each other.

The women's rights movement and the fight for reproductive rights were gaining steam as well.

In New York City, 1968 saw the longest teachers strike in its history, following an educational experiment perpetrated by city officials. This experiment was called "decentralization." With this action, the top politicians in the five boroughs turned over the education of the city's children to a consortium of local community school boards. The justifications behind this move were to give community leaders a seat at the table, concluding that an educational investment in their own community would bear fruit, and that educators of the same ethnic background could better educate students in the neighborhoods.

Race relations in general in New York City were being affected by the contagion of racial divisiveness. The rise of the Black Power movement (which peaked during this year), the Black Pride movement, and numerous race riots across the country contributed to the unease. As a result, later in that same year one school board in a predominantly minority neighborhood in Brooklyn dismissed several teachers and administrators—all white. Albert Shanker, president of the United Federation of Teachers, the union representing New York City public school employees, called a strike. These educators were terminated without due process, but the larger issue became one of minority community control, especially when it came to hiring and firing personnel. Under the Taylor Law, which governs strikes by civil servants in New York City, for each day a teacher was out on the picket line, two days' pay would be extracted. Those teachers opposing union politics chose to cross the picket lines while their counterparts (fellow union teachers) took the financial hit for the action. The strike lasted from the start of the new school term until November 19.

The strike failed on several counts. Firstly, it failed to constrain the city from expanding decentralization by adding to the number of school boards citywide. Every district began to recreate their boards with local control from community members. Thirty-two districts were formed and consisted of only elementary and middle schools. High schools were under the direction and guidance of a centralized high school division, and not part of any local control. Secondly, it convinced those non-striking teachers that union membership was unnecessary, since they received the benefits of the union contract for which their colleagues sacrificed. Finally, the establishment of the school boards began a thirty-year journey into an educational abyss.

The school boards were comprised of barely educated, influential tough activists from the neighborhood who knew next to nothing about education and how to work with kids and teachers. School board elections were conducted in every district, but the credibility and qualifications of these folks varied dramatically from neighborhood to neighborhood.

The decentralized boards became hotbeds for political favoritism, nepotism, graft, corruption, embezzlement, and racism.

In December 1969, the U.S. draft was eliminated in favor of a military lottery. Each date on the calendar was pulled out of a hat and given a number. Those men unlucky enough to have a low number picked based on their birth date were certainly going to war. This led to an increased emigration to Canada, a surge in applications to the National Guard, and a further exodus of corporate men to the classroom.

You would think that experiencing this explosive and poisonous time in history would serve to scare me away from taking on a teaching career, no less in a very dangerous inner-city neighborhood in the South Bronx, nicknamed Fort Apache, after the police precinct assigned to that district.

On the contrary, it was in this exact environment that my teaching career began to take form.

Chapter 2 – One Starry Optimist

While New York City was experimenting with decentralization, I was spending my senior year of college in Seville, Spain, on a study abroad program sponsored by Queens College.

The maternal side of my family spoke an ancient language called Ladino, having immigrated from Istanbul and Ismir, Turkey. Ladino was a combination of Castilian Spanish, Hebrew, Greek, Turkish, and other language elements. I found it interesting that my major in Spanish allowed me to understand this language of my ancestors. Spending a year in Spain would allow me to immerse myself in the language I planned to teach and give me a good idea of the history of the Sephardic Jews whom King Ferdinand and Queen Isabella of Spain forced out during the Inquisition of 1492 under threat of execution.

While I thought that I had left turmoil behind when I left the States, I was surprised to learn that I was exchanging one educational extreme for another.

The Franco era in Spain was one of intellectual constraints. Guardia Civil police officers on horseback, armed with machine guns, lined the campus of the University of Seville on a daily basis to ensure that censorship of intellectual writings dictated by the government would be maintained. Nevertheless, several of the professors had us purchase the books on Spanish history and literature, which had been banned by the government, in underground basements and alleyways from black market dealers. Even though I left behind a chaotic school system, I was beginning to appreciate my freedom in the U.S. The schools in Spain, on the other hand, had very strict limitations on what could be taught in their classrooms.

When I returned from my studies abroad at the end of 1971, I encountered an educational system in New York City little changed from when I left. Having completed my educational requirements to become a Spanish teacher, I felt fortunate to secure a teaching position in a Title One middle school in Fort Apache, The Bronx. A Title One school was then one in which more than two-thirds of the students fell below the threshold set by the federal government to be considered impoverished. This designation of poverty meant that I would be working with a student body that lived in the most abysmal conditions. With peeling lead paint, roach and rat infestations, lack of heat in the winter, and not a hint of air conditioning in the heat of summer, the kids came from neighborhoods that looked more like bombed-out Germany after the war than a safe haven in which to grow. In the absence of nutritional meals, health, dental, and optical care, these kids were challenged before they even got to school.

When I was interviewed for the job, I was told that I was the twelfth substitute teacher to hold this position in the six weeks since school began; the last surviving only one week. My youth and naivete prevented me from considering the implications of this last statement. And so, my first day began. I was scared shitless! To begin, entering the classroom so late in the term was a negative, since I knew that reversing poor discipline and poor management from the previous eleven teachers would be a real challenge.

I survived the cursing, the racist remarks, the chairs being thrown at my head, and the total abrogation of the responsibilities of several helpless administrators to curtail such action, only to find upon starting the ignition in my car at the end of the day that my battery had been stolen during school hours. Fortunately, I'm a quick learner, and found out that the guy on the corner who stole the battery was nice enough to sell it back to me for $50! I hadn't even received my first paycheck and I already had a negative balance in my account. At least the hoods on the block did not steal the car. As an aside, four years later, my car was stolen. When the automatic ignition cutoff engaged, the thieves had to abandon the car. When I located the car down the block, it had been ticketed for illegal parking! I desperately wanted to teach, so putting up with this "minor" inconvenience was part of my initiation. Wow, so you wanna be a teacher...

The next morning, I ran into a colleague who, in all of his optimism, insisted that I was wasting my time trying to educate "these animals," so I needn't even try. To say that I was shocked at this comment is an understatement. We were, after all, educators. He followed up this remark by berating me for wearing a jacket and tie to work. Another of his pals took my tie, wrapped it around my neck, and told me to get rid of this "fucking" thing. After all, I was the youngest teacher on the staff, still had my baby face, and you could spot me a mile away. They saw me coming. I refused to get discouraged.

I soon learned that this was the mindset of a significantly large group of disgruntled teachers who, by the very nature of this thinking, were setting the kids up for failure. I vowed to avoid them and prove them wrong. Luckily, I was embraced by a much smaller core group of like-minded educators who believed that we had to change the culture of the school in order to survive. Failure was not an option. These kids deserved strong, caring teachers who were willing to work hard to defy the stereotypes that had followed them throughout their school career thus far. The best advice that I received by my positive child-centered colleagues was to stay far away from the teachers' lounge where all the bitching and moaning about the kids and the administrators would take place.

The new principal of the school was a tough and demanding administrator. He was also a motivator who turned around this proverbial "Blackboard Jungle."

This man who hired me had high expectations and instituted a zero-tolerance policy regarding attendance, punctuality, and behavior, not just for the students, but also for staff. His out-of-the-box thinking led him to create teaching clusters, wherein a group of four teachers, one in each major discipline, became responsible for one group of approximately 128 students. The benefits of this grouping were extraordinary. Firstly, the students knew that they were responsible to these four teachers. Secondly, the teachers were able to follow the same students throughout the year, making it much easier to confer with each other regarding disciplinary, academic, or home life issues.

This networking provided a more intimate relationship with each student, with major crossover, similar to a team of doctors working with the same patients. The support provided to these students was further advanced by the school resource team who followed up on issues that required further action by mental health professionals or social workers. Lastly, the cluster teachers generally shared the same educational philosophy, classroom management skills, and standards of success-oriented teaching, allowing them to become a stronger unit.

This successful concept led the school to be designated a "model school" in the district, and our leader was named the Principal of the Year.

Having a good track record does not necessarily bring longevity. In fact, in many instances, it creates exactly the opposite reaction. So, after just two successful years for me working at the school, I had to say "adios" to our boss, who was given a promotion. The culture of our organization was most likely going to change, and hopefully become even better. I was extremely fond of our departed principal, but now having a greater voice in the entire district, we were not totally saying goodbye.

Our new principal was experienced and was known by the faculty, having worked in our building as a supervisor. The teachers were concerned that we would be getting someone from outside of the district who was a designee of the recently created community school boards. Fortunately, that was not the case. We were happy with their choice. As I have mentioned previously, the local school boards were rife with poorly educated neighborhood residents who used their position to reward those who supported them. Under the local school boards, appointment lists, seniority regulations, hiring, firing, and budgeting fell under their auspices. In general, the board members did as they wished without regard for due process and qualifications.

Previously, official appointments for teaching and administrative positions for middle and elementary schools were taken from a central board list managed for the entire city. This list consisted of all the candidates who passed their licensing exams and were appointed to schools in chronological order. Under decentralization, local school district boards were given this task, and the legitimacy of their placements was questionable especially in the case of supervisory positions. As a result, numerous people were given management jobs in the district and/or in the schools without the necessary qualifications. In absence of any meaningful oversight the local board members who were not qualified themselves to make these decisions selected their cronies for these jobs. The board members in every district most often were chosen based on their ethnicity, which represented the residents of those neighborhoods. In some communities the board members were very qualified depending on their education, experience working with schools, and participation in civic affairs, while in other places this was not the case.

One such appointee, a former physical education teacher from another place in another district with little administrative experience, took over the principalship in one of their schools. The belief of several boards under the decentralized schools was that black students would identify best with a black leader. Under our previous administrator, who was black himself, color was never an issue. He ran the school with academic scholarship as number one on his priority list. Good teachers were praised and recognized for their achievements. No one made an issue of ethnicity, which should not play a role in his evaluation in any case. He was an extraordinary leader, and we all valued him for his great service to the children and staff.

Our former principal had an open-door policy for teachers and students, walked the halls to make certain that no one was cutting class, and made sure that the classrooms were functioning with learning taking place. Our new administrator had a warmer approach to staff and gave the assistant principals and teachers more autonomy in participating in school affairs. My friends who were teachers in other schools complained that their principals were unprepared for the job and that their leaders had to call upon their "helpers" to put out fires, find solutions for crises, and outline next steps. This lack of understanding and inability to provide direction for the staff and students were often ignored because of the camaraderie with the local school board. This situation became more widespread and led to a total breakdown in school culture throughout the city. Fortunately, this contagious atmosphere did not reach our school, but hearing about these incidents made me feel very uncomfortable.

As the days passed, I began to sense some changes in the work ethic of the staff. The beauty of the cluster component began to disintegrate as teachers felt unappreciated and demoralized by actions of the local board. Soon, the more dedicated ones began to leave the school in exponential numbers. In some cases their replacements were poorly equipped to meet the challenges of a tough, inner-city middle school in a deteriorating neighborhood. More than half of the administrators in the building were trying to assist the teachers with discipline, but when it was discovered that several did not have supervisory licenses, they lost the respect of many teachers and other administrators who had the appropriate qualifications. These teachers who were pulled out of the classroom to serve as supervisors without administrative degrees sent out a negative message to the staff.

This practice was obviously something that the district allowed, and these staff members were often friends of school board members. In most schools it was the principal who made this decision. The high schools, however, were monitored more closely, and their budgets were scrutinized to make sure that administrative positions were not created at the expense of teaching placements. These citywide regulations did not permit teachers from being excused from their classrooms full-time to be supervisors without the qualifications or official appointments. Sadly, in the elementary and middle schools this practice was very common because the local boards were autonomous in hiring personnel.

Decentralization was created in an attempt to do away with a large-scale bureaucracy by giving each district local control over the schools. Community activists and interested parents rightfully believed that they were the only people who could truly be sensitive to the needs of their kids, especially in a diverse city of over one million children. As a result, however, no one was prepared for this sudden change, and unqualified, inexperienced folks engaged in a power grab for local board seats. Previously, district personnel and certainly supervisory staff had to adhere to civil service regulations.

There was an incredible price to pay once board members were given complete autonomy in making decisions for the education of thousands of kids. Millions of dollars were put into the hands of community folks who did not know what to do with the money. Again, the success and failure of this new arrangement varied from district to district.

The results of a disconnected school board that now applied their own hiring rules continued to tear at the fabric of our institution. Now that the intermediate and elementary schools became decentralized, I am not even sure if central headquarters in Brooklyn knew what was going on in the local districts.

While there was war around us, there was war within us.

Chapter 3 — How Are the Children?

In the teaching profession, we very often get caught up with sifting through state mandates, district mandates, and the chancellor's memoranda, and we forget about the big picture, the kids. It is so important to remind ourselves of the famous African greeting of the Masai Tribe: "How are the children?" When the Masai people greet each other, they begin with this question, to which the response is always, "All the children are well." Their children always come first. In our most advanced cities, sadly, the students are very often the last ones to be considered in complying with any educational mandate.

The notion of the affective domain describes the idea that before you even attempt to educate kids and teach them academics, you need to succeed in building mutual respect.

Tough love is not exclusively relegated to a parent/child relationship. *Tough love*, with regard to education, means showing respect, giving respect, setting limits, setting goals, being consistent, and having high expectations—even higher than they'd dare to dream. Working with kids is like creating a partnership. In the creation of this partnership, as educators, we are often called upon to play the role of parent, social worker, guidance counselor, and psychologist.

Most of my colleagues felt that they needed to be confrontational rather than sensitive, thereby compromising the exact relationship they were attempting to establish. For many members of the teaching staff, working in the South Bronx was like being in an extremely unfamiliar world. Aside from skin color and language, the inner-city neighborhood was a stark contrast to the life experiences that many of us had, even when it came to clothing, slang, music, and way of life. The middle school concept added another layer of difficulty, in that we were dealing with impending puberty, neighborhood gang activity, dysfunctional family situations, and, very often, poor medical care. Unfortunately, if these experiences are not taken into consideration in your daily lesson planning, kids will not be able to identify with and totally comprehend the subject matter. We needed to draw parallels to their circumstances and make the content relevant.

Home visits to the housing projects, which fed our school, became commonplace for me. I needed to earn the trust of the family as well as the child. Let's not forget that in the 1970s we didn't have cell phones, many of the students did not have landlines, letters sent home were often confiscated before they reached the parent, and English was a second language for many. I had no choice but to make face-to-face contact with some family member in order to have some kind of communication about the child's progress. It was extremely rare for a teacher in NYC to make a home visit. For me it was a *calling*. Since my wife and I were both raised in similar neighborhoods in the Bronx, going into a poorly lit high-rise and stepping into an elevator that smelled of urine didn't seem to frighten me. Fortunately today, most parents have cell phones, and communicating with them is much easier. Previously it was nearly impossible to contact the parent during their workday, but now you can get to the guardian just about anywhere, anytime.

I realized that changes needed to be made to my own teaching practices to provide additional supports for these children. It suddenly occurred to me that although these kids lived in the city, they had absolutely no exposure to anything the metropolis had to offer because they never left their familiar streets. This realization became apparent to me one day while teaching a lesson. The conversation came up about Broadway shows when I happened to mention that I had seen one during the weekend. The students gave me a blank stare since they never had this experience. So, I decided to give them the opportunity to attend a real live performance.

I asked the parents to sign off on a late-day consent (perhaps as late as six o'clock in the evening) so that we could attend a matinee show. I collected twenty-five cents per week until we had enough money to buy tickets to *Ain't Misbehavin'*. Of course, I prepped the kids for months about their behavior in the theater and on the subway, threatening them with the *kiss of death* if they failed to cooperate or embarrass me. We traveled by subway from the Bronx to Times Square—sixty kids, their eyes popping out of their heads at the neon signs and hordes of people traversing the Square. They sat glued to their seats throughout the show. Each and every one of them thanked me for giving them an experience they likely would not have had.

As an aside, my daughter, who is an elementary school Special Education teacher in Queens, took her class many years ago to a bowling alley to enhance their mathematics experience with something fun. After all, what better way to learn basic number principles than to keep score in a bowling alley! When they sat down at the lanes, my daughter asked them to choose a comfortable ball. They were puzzled. They couldn't imagine why the balls had three holes. Again, we cannot assume that our normal is the same normal for those we teach. By the way, understanding these cultural differences is even more important today since the immigrant population in the city is greater than ever.

I also realized that so many of my students had family members from countries around the world. Rather than ignoring this valuable resource, I chose to use the diversity in my class as a means to embrace the entire school community.

My classes produced a foreign language magazine, entitled *The Intercontinental*. It was a multicultural and multilingual magazine featuring personal experiences about my students' native lands. It included movie reviews of English-language and foreign films, stories about artists in the music industry, artwork, and recipes from their homelands. The purpose this project served was not only to expand the students' ability to communicate in English, Spanish, and French—the three languages taught in the school—but also to create a culture of inclusion for the large Spanish-speaking population who felt disenfranchised from their own learning environment.

We held international food festivals, encouraging our now multicultural students to appreciate the foods of each ethnicity.

And then there was Connie.... My darling Connie was a student in my seventh grade Spanish class. Some students have a certain spark, a special connection, a tug at your heart. Yes, Connie had it all. One day, Connie noticed that I was struggling to teach, as I had a bad cold. She told me I needed a good cup of tea. I told her that I hated tea. No matter, she bought me a cup of tea on her lunch break and refused to leave until she saw me down the whole cup. This was a kindness I rarely experienced in this building.

Today, fifty years later, Connie is a public health nurse dedicating each day to improving the lives of so many people. Even then, she showed the compassion of an adult who saw not the color of your skin, but the goodness of the heart.

Still, today, Connie calls me regularly. She continues to refer to me as "Dad" and never forgets my birthday or fails to leave me a Father's Day message. Connie continues to generate love wherever she goes.

As coincidences go, years later, Connie's daughter enrolled as a student in the high school where I was assigned as a teacher and administrator.

Do not misunderstand me; I like to highlight the positive before I talk about the negative. Teaching at this school was no walk in the park. We had kids with criminal records, who had been so physically and emotionally damaged that we were wholly inadequate when it came to providing them with the resources necessary to even begin to educate them. The one school psychologist, who was often shared with two other schools, had such an impossible workload that he barely spent ten minutes with the student. Mental health has always been the stepchild of the Board of Education's budgetary allowance.

To this point, in the early 1980s, a man was attacked in the subway station in Manhattan by four men who were intent on robbing him. When I read the report, I was deeply saddened to learn that, aside from the hideous attack, one of the attackers had been a student of mine six years earlier.

In spite of the positive outcomes that I was generating within my individual school experience, the combination of a number of district administrators making poor decisions in hiring and the departure of some of my fellow teachers and supervisors, I was becoming more and more uneasy about my job. I was extremely glad, however, that my working relationship with my principal continued to flourish.

In 1978, while this transition was taking place, I was completing my courses at Hofstra University, which would lead to New York State certification as a public school administrator.

In the spring of 1983, I was awarded the New York City license as a middle school and elementary school assistant principal. It was my hope that once I become certified, I would be able to move up as a supervisor in my school, and assist in the making of an exemplary educational environment in the district that would be noted for success. However, it quickly became clear to me that after discussions with school board officials I had no future in this school, not as a teacher nor as an administrator. I was very surprised since I had received two awards as Teacher of the Year from the district and had been praised for my performance working in their afterschool programs. I was well known in these surroundings. Educational leaders in the neighborhood knew me by my first name.

I thought this moment would be the appropriate time to meet with my principal to extend to her my interest in joining her administrative staff. With all of my certifications, two master's degrees, and the equivalent of a doctorate, I felt more qualified than ever to make a difference in this middle school. My principal acknowledged that she was pleased with my work, and that I was great with the kids. In fact, she met with my

Hofstra supervisor regarding my progress and required fieldwork as an administrative intern in the school and had glowing things to say about me. Sadly, she could not help me in spite of all the accolades. No explanation or reason was given to me as to why my offer to join the administrative team was not being considered.

This entire experience was becoming a nightmare. I was terribly disappointed and very naive in thinking that I would be welcomed with open arms by my offer. Yet I knew in my heart that this decision was not hers to make. We continued to have a good working relationship and mutual respect for each other. However, my career plans and dreams had to be revised.

Chapter 4 – A Hidden Quota System

After ten years of working under the current principal and two with the principal who had hired me, I decided it was time to move on. With twelve years of teaching experience and a New York State certification as an administrator, the moment for me to take on a new challenge seemed to be approaching.

For the past five years, I had noticed that many of my colleagues began to take on a very negative approach to kids and parents. They became resentful and conveyed to me that they were nothing but pawns in the district game whose goal was to use cronyism in their hiring practices for the schools. I always seemed to think of myself as an exception because both principals sent kudos my way regarding my work and relationship with kids, parents, and staff. When I inquired at the personnel office as to why I could not be considered for an administrative position, I was given responses on a number of occasions that led me to think that it was because of my race.

Calls to the union in the district confirmed my thoughts. In fact, conversations with a number of folks in charge of hiring in other districts indicated that white administrators would have a very tough time getting promoted in certain neighborhoods where more persons of color were being recruited. I was told that this practice was similar to a quota system, and that I was in the wrong place at the wrong time. I was shocked to hear similar responses, especially from local authorities who knew about my dedication to the children every day. As shocked as I was to hear these comments, which were related to race, I began to realize how the black and brown populations in our country had felt for years, having experienced much hidden and subtle acts of discrimination in employment. Sadly, this practice continues today in many industries. This feeling of being disenfranchised allowed me to understand some of the pain that others had to confront. This incident certainly helped me to be more sensitive and aware in the future.

Perhaps I had been very blind and refused to recognize the signs sent out in the district that the growing culture and bureaucracy were not conducive to promoting academic progress. The kids were certainly not considered a priority. This next situation was even more explosive and terribly demoralizing, and should have been a wake-up call for me that it was time to begin a new journey. I was called at home the second week of July by the superintendent overseeing summer programs asking me to work in their reading program. I jumped at the opportunity because this badly needed income would help me pay my bills until the next regular paycheck on September 16.

However, given my honesty and moral compass I reminded this administrator that I did not have seniority or what was called retention rights. I did not want to violate union regulations and deny another employee a summer job. His response was that I was desperately needed, and this issue would not be a problem. I quickly got dressed and drove an hour to the South Bronx to begin working. Little did I know that the next six weeks would go downhill and prove disastrous to my future career plans. I was assigned two reading classes and was told that I would supervise two paraprofessionals in the program.

The next day came, and the "paras" arrived two hours late. We had a conversation about their schedule, and they promised to arrive on time the next day. Nevertheless, over the next several days they continued to ignore my requests, so I felt it was time to bring this problem to the principal's attention. Sadly, I realized that my complaint was not taken seriously when I overheard the principal tell his para friends to ignore my directions to arrive on time. I felt defeated and knew all too well the dangers of cronyism. Conducting business in a professional manner became secondary.

The situation blew up even further when I was informed the following week that I was being *bumped* by a more senior person. In the middle of the day I was sent home. I was extremely depressed and disappointed, especially since I had been making progress with my bilingual youngsters, who were beginning to show improved skills in reading and writing. They had only days left to prepare for the State exams given in August. Two weeks went by, and I received the call again to return to my job, as there might have been a mistake in hiring.

Again, I ran to the South Bronx, to the same school, only to find out that the staff did not even know that I had been gone. Obviously, the left hand did not know what the right hand was doing. I continued working alone since my assistants were worthless and were concerned with making parties and celebrations for fellow staff members while ignoring the kids. The loss of instructional time was terribly upsetting, but no one seemed to care, especially the administrators and decision-makers in the district. In fact, there seemed to be more supervisors walking around without administrative licenses than teachers in the classrooms.

Several ironic situations followed when, after being reprimanded for a number of insignificant issues in my teaching, I was informed that I would be receiving a certificate for excellence as Outstanding Teacher of Summer Programs. This was followed by the receipt of a letter from the district two months later informing me that I was in violation of summer school regulations by taking a job from a more senior person and that I would be banned from ever working in summer school again. I was in shock, but not surprised. Millions of dollars in state aid and district monies were wasted because of poor decisions made by uncaring administrators, not to mention the tremendous loss to many needy students who had to pass exit exams at the end of the summer. Again, all of these very detrimental outcomes were directly related to the hiring practices in this district. I had to get out of "Dodge."

For years I had ignored the signs and rumors of corruption in these surroundings. I had heard stories about stolen pianos and extravagant staff development excursions to the Caribbean. All these pieces of the puzzle started to fall into place, painting a nasty picture of this environment. I was beginning to get infected by the virus. I was no longer immune to everything going on around me even in my own classroom with the windows and doors closed shut.

Fortunately, today the budgets are more closely monitored since the days of decentralization as we knew it. This trend lasted for thirty years and finally ended in 2003. Today local board members participate in the decisions influencing programs offered in schools, but major budgetary and hiring practices are left to more qualified administrative leaders. Parents are on school leadership teams, but their involvement is limited to advisement. The mayor and city hall are much more involved in the major decisions influencing the schools.

However, recent disputes between the governor and mayor regarding control of the 1,800 schools in New York City have added to the bureaucracy. No one is clear as to who has the final word regarding major decisions and school policy. In many suburban schools outside of the city board members are elected to their positions, and are very influential in the decisions regarding budget, personnel, and instruction. In the city the extent of participation varies dramatically from district to district and often comes down to who screams the loudest to get things done. One school in Manhattan recently collected $50,000 thanks to the efforts of the Parents Association, while many other schools do not even have an active parent group at all. My daughter teaches in Queens and she struggles to get parents to attend conferences regarding the progress of their own kids.

At this point all of my closer friends had transferred to other schools. My cluster group had dissolved. The tone of the school was untenable. I truly enjoyed working with my principal, and I would have loved to stay and participate as a team member in her supervisory cabinet. Now I hated going to work each day, not because of the relationship with my leader, which was excellent, but because of the people outside of the school who set the rules for hiring, and who poisoned the environment. I felt that I was no longer being judged by this school district purely on my performance and relationship with kids. For my own sanity, I had to get out. I submitted my transfer papers.

I had this naive notion that once the papers were received by my principal, all would go smoothly, and that I would say a courteous "goodbye," leaving her to deal with the rules that were promoted by the local board. I was wrong. I even thought that she might change her mind and reconsider my proposal to serve in an administrative position, rather than lose me. Again, I was wrong. When she received my written request to leave she could not sign off. It was really my misunderstanding in thinking that anyone could request a transfer.

I complained to the district about not being permitted to transfer and was told by the office staff that "certain" teachers were not being given releases because the district could not attract "certain" teachers to the local schools as replacements. The explanation that I was given was their response to an attempt to keep the district ethnically and racially balanced. It was clear to me that "certain" referred to my being "white."

My principal was prevented from signing off on my transfer due to local board decisions. I came home that day totally depressed. Could I really be prevented from leaving? After all, this wasn't a jail sentence and, if in fact it was, I had served more than my time. I felt like a prisoner. If I couldn't get that transfer, I was considering leaving education altogether. I would rather flip hamburgers than continue to be an enabler of this unacceptable behavior by district leaders. I had a purpose in life. I was disconsolate. I am convinced that my principal was saddened to hear that I wanted to leave since I had been at the school for a long time.

For all the negative comments I've heard over the years regarding unions, and I've heard them all, there are important reasons for their existence. With unfair labor practices being executed in the workplace in many schools, there was good cause for labor leaders to get involved. As a lifetime member of the United Federation of Teachers (UFT), I called upon them to intervene on my behalf. The only advice they could give me at that time was to apply for a UFT transfer.

Job openings in education were advertised in several ways. I had seen a position posted on a transfer list in a school in District Four in Manhattan. This job was included on a citywide Board of Education list of borough-wide positions made available. The UFT had its own list of UFT transfer opportunities. Transfers through this listing could be made without cause, as long as the number of school transfer requests was under a certain percentage of the school's staffing population. If the requirements were met the principals could not block the applicants from leaving once the requests were approved. This practice is the backbone of a union's worth, to help members who are unfairly targeted; to use their clout to deter what was blatantly unfair action on the part of the personnel office. Even though the UFT did not know me or help me personally, the anonymous transfer list was designed to allow for a small percentage of teachers to move from one district to another.

Today, however, it is very difficult to transfer if you have more than ten years of experience. Budgeting rules have changed and now teacher salaries dictate how much of the school budget it will cost to hire each staff member. Veteran teachers earning higher salaries cost the school more money. Principals in many cases prefer to hire inexperienced people because they literally cost less. This practice is very sad. Previously, all teachers regardless of experience cost the same amount. Each teacher was equivalent to one teaching unit in the budget rather than a dollar amount. The number of students enrolled in the school determined how many teaching units a principal would receive in the budget.

Over the years many bureaucratic and antiquated practices governing the schools in an incredibly diverse city have led to proposals to break up the educational system into five boroughs. Any movement to accomplish this structural change has gone nowhere. Many residents still feel that the largest school system in the country has become too unmanageable.

I applied for the transfer to a middle school knowing that I was competing with many others for the same job. Miraculously, my application was accepted and approved. It was a shot in the dark. For my friends and family, it became an inside joke that I got a promotion from Fort Apache, the Bronx, to "glorious" East Harlem. For years the people with whom I shared this newly found fortune shuddered at the thought of me working in either of these places, but for me, it was a welcome change.

After twelve years in the Bronx, I was finally far away from what my district leaders so haughtily called *certain* teachers, and from what I considered to be a *quota system.*

Yes, I was ecstatic about the prospect of starting anew with hopes of restoring my faith in the profession and, at the same time, reigniting my passion for teaching very needy kids. However, I was still very torn.

It sounds hard to believe, but I was actually sorry to leave my school. True, my skills were no longer valued, and I was underappreciated in the district, not to mention looked at as the guy who seemed to be in the wrong place at the wrong time. Yet, this school was my home away from home. My principal and I were good friends, and we parted amicably. She thanked me for my work but couldn't help me with a supervisory placement. Many of the children put a daily smile on my face, and a number of parents were truly thankful for my dedication to their kids. My darling Connie was one of many students who did come to value the caring teachers and the education they were receiving in spite of the negative culture in the district that they were probably too young to even understand.

I do have to acknowledge that I was leaving the school with many years of excellent classroom management skills under my belt. I didn't receive combat pay, but I did experience the challenge of a lifetime and, because of that challenge, I was leaving very well prepared to work anywhere with any type of student.

Middle school kids are the toughest bunch, not to mention that they are also inner-city teenagers. The notion of "survival of the fittest" certainly applied to the entire staff in this Bronx school. Some simply survived to last another day. Others survived to understand the need for individualized instruction based on the unique needs and backgrounds of the students. In fact, I came to realize years later that the weakest teachers with whom I worked when I arrived at the high school level were often the ones who never really experienced tough educational challenges in their early teaching career. They had never been called upon to be creative in incorporating ways to overcome the many deficits with which our students presented themselves. Tough kids make for tough teachers. I appreciated these last few years working in very stressful surroundings since my newly acquired skills were transferrable. Man, I was truly grateful for the time spent in one of the most difficult districts in the city.

I was so fortunate to even land a position in 1971 with so many men taking up spots to avoid the draft. I was so grateful early on to my first principal, who was a demanding, no-nonsense African American guy with tremendous dedication and love for kids. Sadly, he left after two years, received a promotion, and was later criticized and removed maybe because he was so smart and had great insight. But for me, anyway, he taught me more in his short stay than many other supervisors did in ten years. He was truly inspirational. I learned what educators call "survival skills," which proved to benefit me greatly in the coming years especially working in tough neighborhoods. Yet, I paid a very high price for these rewards with twelve years of dedication. I was departing with a feeling of very little respect and very little sincere recognition.

Finally, the camaraderie of many fellow colleagues, at least in the early years, kept me alive, since we were on the same page. Luckily for me, two of them were already working in the Manhattan school to which I was now being assigned. I could not wait to join them, yet my heart was heavy, and my eyes were filled with tears as I left the South Bronx.

I have to share with you that I really did feel let down. I felt a sense of failure because I truly wanted to be an administrator in my first school, and I knew in my heart that I would have been successful in returning it to the golden days of being the number one junior high in the district. I never would have imagined that perhaps the color of my skin would have been used by local officials as a criterion for promotion nor as a means to keep me in this place indefinitely. Again, I learned a really good lesson, and promised myself that if given the opportunity, I would strive to change the current methods used in hiring personnel for teaching or administrative positions. I finally accepted the fact that I did not have a future in this school. Little did I know, however, that this change would be a blessing in disguise. I soon realized that I had died and gone to heaven as I moved into East Harlem, New York.

Chapter 5 – I Died and
Went to Heaven

In the summer of 1983, my luck began to change. The superintendent and deputy of District Four in Manhattan called to interview me once the UFT transfer became official. There was one additional individual at the table, the principal of a new high school in East Harlem. He wanted me to join the staff of this experimental school, The Manhattan Center for Science and Mathematics (MCSM) on the Benjamin Franklin Campus. Not coincidentally, this organization was the very school to which two of my former middle school colleagues had transferred. In a matter of minutes, I was hired.

The excitement was just too overwhelming. This offer was much more than I had expected. It was really a big deal.

As I walked through the streets of this Latino enclave in East Harlem, known as the *barrio*, the sounds of activity and civilization gave me the right shot of adrenaline to reset my entire existence. The local church bells, the shopkeepers opening their stores, the smells of bakeries with coal ovens, and carts with shaved ice generated a new sensation, much like moving into a new home. I left behind my former intermediate school in the Bronx, which had been built under the elevated train tracks. The noise from the trains was a distracting force, and the danger from above was ever-present, as the kids would throw soda cans and bottles from the platforms. During the winter months, snowballs became the weapon of choice, as the kids used staff for target practice. At Halloween, we were *egged* as we left the building. Any sense of community on the surrounding streets was obstructed by my vision of abandoned apartments with boarded-up windows and doors.

These memories still left a very bad taste in my mouth. I always maintained that teachers and staff of Title I schools housed in these dilapidated neighborhoods should receive battle pay, but that is a conversation for another day. Yes, I was ready to make MCSM and the rich and vibrant sounds of life and energy in this new *hood* my home away from home for the foreseeable future.

Manhattan Center for Science and Mathematics (MCSM) was a unique experiment in that it was a collaboration between District Four in East Harlem and the High School Division of the Board of Education. Given this new partnership, it was understood, perhaps in the form of a gentleman's agreement, that traditional regulations that governed the functioning of high schools were waived. However, it remained to be seen how much autonomy would be given to this pilot program, especially in terms of allowing the school to accept students from anywhere in the city. We were no longer a traditional zoned high school.

Here, kids from any neighborhood in New York City could attend this experimental high school, which opened with only a ninth-grade class and was intended to grow yearly into a four-grade, fully functioning secondary school.

Teachers were recruited primarily from District Four based on their middle school experience and were selected based on their claim to fame in the district. Much like an actor auditioning for a play, standout teachers were easily recognizable within the local region.

Teachers were asked to buy into the school culture, which, being a new school, was fairly opaque. As part of our mission and vision for the school we were proposing to take in marginal kids whose reading and math scores were on grade level or perhaps even one to two years below grade level. These kids were on the fence academically, but with the help of a nurturing school environment, we believed that we could prepare them for college. Knowing full well that many of the students who would be attending the school would be deficient in numerous academic areas, would be coming from homes that lacked support, and would be coming from neighborhoods whose schools classified them as uneducable, our hope and expectation was to make these kids competitive.

This was truly revolutionary for New York City. Historically, children born and raised in most neighborhoods were limited to attending high schools with proven track records of repeated failure. There was absolutely no choice available to these kids to attend a school outside of their zip code other than applying for the specialized high schools that required an admissions test or talent portfolio. These testing schools reached a very tiny percentage of city kids and have traditionally admitted very few children of color even until this day. Considering that seventy percent of the kids in the city are kids of color, recently fewer than ten black children were accepted into the highly acclaimed Stuyvesant High

School. What's wrong with this picture? Perhaps unintentionally, these restrictions re-created the very segregated schools that the Supreme Court previously had ordered desegregated.

This chance of a lifetime was a golden opportunity for any student who had an interest in math, science, or technology to attend a high school other than the one in their zoned location. Kids were told from the onset that part of the agreement in accepting a placement at our school meant that they would have an additional period of instruction daily. The students were truly self-selected in their willingness to work harder and take on a greater concentration in the sciences. After my long journey in the Bronx, coming to this school district and hearing this news was a far cry from my previous experience.

In addition, I had also been informed that when the original blueprint and groundwork for the creation of this school were shared with the Latino parents in the community who represented over 60 percent of the population, the proposal was rejected. Apparently, plans were being considered for a bilingual high school, and the parents overwhelmingly cast their vote instead for a college preparation math and science school. I felt as though I had died and gone to heaven. The number of immigrant parents, many of whom were from the Caribbean and Central and South America, who recognized the value of an education and wanted to be part of the decision-making process astounded me. I became part of a new stratosphere.

Considering that MCSM was created to replace the school that the city took over, which was the failing Benjamin Franklin Campus High School, the stakes were extraordinarily high for its success. The risks taken with this monumental change to the way kids applied to high school, coupled with the special permission we received from the High School Division of the Board of Education, cannot be overstated. Ironically, even though we opened our doors to the entire city, the first ninth-grade class consisted of only 147 children, the majority of whom came from the surrounding neighborhoods. To be clear, MCSM was neither a magnet school nor a charter school, and perhaps in absence of those designations, attracting kids to this new school was not easy at first.

The Isaac Newton Middle School provided a good number of our freshman students. Housed in the same building as MCSM, along with River East Elementary School, our campus was an even wider experiment in education. It was most unusual for an elementary school, middle school, and high school to share facilities in one building. Years later we added a preschool. This proximity of educational levels proved to be more important than anyone could have anticipated. Being surrounded by children ages three to eighteen was truly exciting and unique. Seeing the big kids sitting with the little kids in the cafeteria and for special events sent chills up my spine. No one outside of this community could believe that this joint effort had a chance to work.

I arrived at MCSM in August 1983, the second year of this educational experiment. I began working as a ninth-grade Spanish teacher. I was immediately shocked by the stark differences between my middle school experience and this new high school environment. The male staff members were sporting jackets and ties, as opposed to the ripped jeans and T-shirts worn in my last school. Instead of walking through the halls with bats and yardsticks, these teachers moved through the hallways with notebooks and lesson plans. The entire atmosphere appeared calm. It was like a family environment where teachers worked together. Faculty ate lunch with their students. Students were greeted at the door each morning. Every single breath uttered by the MCSM team was about academics. The school's mission and vision of the four-year plan was clearly laid out, with college preparatory initiatives included in each area.

Because we were such a small school at the time, it was the perfect opportunity to create a family-type atmosphere. Our budget was commensurate with our student population. That meant that it was minimal, certainly insufficient to service the students adequately. Teachers voluntarily took on the roles of guidance counselor, social worker, support personnel, and attendance coordinator. This shared responsibility, in itself, was a drastic departure from the mindset of my former school staff, where no one volunteered for anything. If you did offer to take on additional assignments you would be ostracized from the general population for doing more than your contractual duties. You were strongly encouraged to do as little as possible, as little appreciation was shown by the administration or the hostile school board. Sadly, this culture continues to exist in many schools where dedication is not recognized or rewarded. The few hard-working professionals in the organization are considered out of place by their colleagues.

MCSM had a child-centered atmosphere. Work was enjoyable, satisfying, and productive. It created a rebirth in me and reinforced the reasons why I chose teaching as a career.

Chapter 6 – Growing Pains

In 1983, at least for me, the stars seemed to align. After five years of internal struggles within my own head as to whether to leave the Bronx or keep fighting an endless battle to gain recognition and upward mobility, I finally made it *big time*. I was accepted into high school in a new community with professional colleagues who wanted to do right by kids and enjoy their jobs at the same time. What a refreshing new concept! The idea that teachers would actually be motivated to work hard was just unbelievable. As time passed, our program and mission became more and more familiar to the movers and shakers in the city. Before long, visitors to the school included the Reverend Jesse Jackson, Senator Gary Hart, and Senator Patrick Moynihan, who provided their words of inspiration and encouragement to the youngsters. Even more memorable for all of us in the school was the unexpected visit of the singing group Menudo from Puerto Rico. After having lunch with Ricky Martin, I was really living *la vida loca*.

The MCSM family, as we became known, now consisted of a ninth and a tenth grade with approximately thirty faculty members sharing the teaching responsibilities of their own subject area, and also volunteering to take on guidance and mentoring assignments. We were small enough to enjoy a common lunch period with the kids and faculty celebrations during our free time. The Sunshine Fund took care of sad and glad tidings, and we all looked to one another for deeper relationships than what is typical in a traditional school environment. The teacher overseeing this initiative made sure that every staff member received a daily dose of cheer. "Smile for me, darling. We are so lucky to be here with these great kids" were her words as she proceeded to sign the teacher up for an upcoming social gathering. They just couldn't refuse. This very bubbly teacher always kept us on a high note. To me, this warm atmosphere was amazing because in my former life in the Bronx, any free moment I had I took as an opportunity to hide from my colleagues. I had rarely eaten lunch with the students. Besides, being in the crossfire of a food fight, especially with sautéed green peas, was not what I relished.

The faculty at MCSM became extremely compatible, and enjoyed engaging in Halloween dress-ups (once I played the scarecrow from *The Wizard of Oz*), Secret Santa activities, and drama club and Broadway show skits featuring students and teachers acting out the major roles alongside each other. We continued to make our jobs more than just teaching. I took on the role of "Doc" in the school production of *West Side Story*. The kids helped me memorize my lines. Once they realized that I was truly a stand-up guy, they recruited me to be the fall guy at the target practice event at their carnival and as a player on the student/faculty softball team. We all shared a common goal, to help make MCSM a special place in the midst of nationwide mediocrity.

My daily workload consisted of five teaching periods with thirty-four kids in each class. My free periods were largely made up of hall patrols, absentee teacher coverages, attendance and guidance duties, meetings, and conferences that were typical for most educators in the public schools.

I refused to mark papers and/or plan lessons during my breaks in the day, as so much was going on that I just couldn't miss. All the paperwork went home with me, and, thank God, my supportive family allowed me the time to do it. The workday was nonstop and, even though contractually I didn't have to check in until 8:40, I was already in the main office before 7:00 a.m., getting things ready for a long day. Yes, I was trying to make a good impression on my principal and subject supervisors. More than that, I vowed to never forget that I had left my last school by the skin of my teeth, and my job in this school was hanging by a thread. Let me explain.

The High School Division had come to resent our special status because the local District Four continued to claim ownership of our new collaborative by circumventing several citywide regulations. The high schools generally had to follow central headquarters regulations regarding most issues such as hiring, student enrollment, and budget. Manhattan Center was an experimental pilot program given numerous exemptions to these rules as governed by a joint agreement between the local district and the division of high schools.

As time passed central officials began to renege on the original agreement in an attempt to maintain the same status for us as every other high school. There are approximately 250 high schools in the city. We began to experience growing pains on multiple levels. It was truly untimely that the main supporter, who in part helped to conceive Manhattan Center, was asked to take on another job, and we no longer had his open-door policy at our disposal. His track record in the district as a superintendent was extraordinary, but when he was chosen to lead the entire city as chancellor he sadly had a short run. He always had our back with his steadfast defense of our pilot program.

With our protector gone, every move we made was questioned in terms of budget, hiring, licensing, enrollment, and, before long, academic results. Yes, we were expected to make good on this special project. All the naysayers in the District, High School Division, and Central Headquarters had their antennae up and octopus arms out ready to destroy every bit of us once the founding fathers of MCSM were no longer around to defend us. I'll explain later in the chapter the reasons why we were expected to fail.

The faculty at large loved the kids and, of course, we tried to move on—to not pay too much attention to the politics of district leaders who were more concerned over a power play than the success of our students. Maybe we were in denial, but somehow we didn't think that anyone in the city would succeed in closing us up. We were at least determined to continue for four years so that the first graduating class in 1986 would march to the sound of "Pomp and Circumstance" with good academic results and college in sight. The challenges continued to add up. Our experimental program was very much in jeopardy.

First, our visionary was dismissed, then our inaugural principal left. Our beloved assistant principal passed away, and then yet another very dedicated supervisor departed. Even the president of Hunter College, Donna Shalala, who was a major contributor to our school, was leaving for another position. Would we become a regular academic high school just like everyone else, or remain as a collaboration between the decentralized district schools and centralized high schools with certain privileges? The last option would be to close us up altogether. We enjoyed many benefits given to us by Hunter College with access to their campus and library, so the departure of the president, who was a true friend, was a tremendous loss. She had been a major player in the creation of our school and served as a very wise advisor of our educational programs.

Turning back to 1983, after working at MCSM for only six weeks, my immediate supervisor informed me that she had been asked to head up a brand new high school. This person was my greatest advocate and taught me so much in such a short time. She was truly the love of the school. The departure of yet another heavy hitter and supporter of our pilot program was a disappointment just too much to endure, especially since the future of our school was being questioned.

I was distraught, yet my assistant principal was even more distressed. She loved her job at MCSM but more so, she was upset about abandoning her colleagues and the department teachers she supervised. Her major concern was leaving her three departments—Foreign Languages, History, and English—without leadership.

Well, maybe I lost my mind, but I quickly stepped up to the plate and offered to cover these subject areas in her absence. Although I was certified as a New York State High School administrator, I was so new to the school that I was still asking for directions to offices, for help with instructional items, and assistance with school protocols. Yet, in spite of it all, my mentor and advisor accepted my offer. She felt that she knew enough about me and my job performance that she was satisfied I could do the job. My principal agreed. What was I thinking? I had only been at this new school for several weeks and was certainly very wet behind the ears.

Until the semester ended on the 1st of February, I actually continued to teach my five classes, supervise three departments of teachers, and attend administrative meetings. I was literally working morning, noon, and night seven days a week to prove to myself and to everyone else that I could pull off this astronomical feat. Truth be told, I was hanging by a thread. The thread became thinner and thinner as I faced additional pushback within the school and, later, from outside forces.

Internally, I was supervising a number of teachers with higher seniority and greater subject area expertise than myself. In addition, the staff knew that I was serving in an interim acting capacity, meaning that any directives, mandates, or written evaluations that bore my signature could be disputed. My right to this position was being questioned.

Externally, because I had not been officially appointed to my position, any licensed supervisor anywhere in the city could claim the right to my job. Living in this precarious situation, I was working very long days without additional compensation. In those years, interim acting staff didn't receive the same contractual salary as the appointed staff. At one point, my teachers were making a higher salary than me without the administrative headaches that came with the interim acting position. So unfair, but I guess I had to pay my dues.

In the summer of 1986, three years after I took on this interim status, I received a letter from the Department of Personnel and Human Resources at Brooklyn Headquarters to report immediately for placement. Initially, I thought this was a mistake, knowing the number of errors a large educational bureaucracy could make. Nevertheless, somewhere in the back of my mind, I considered that this request was a vindictive move against our school for the unique and very special situation we as a high school enjoyed with the decentralized schools in District Four.

As an experimental school, MCSM had never been endorsed as a legal entity by the Department of Education. Moreover, the Office of Personnel in Brooklyn was not fond of the fact that our principal continued to circumvent seniority laws when it came to hiring the best people for the job. This practice contributed to the many reasons why central headquarters wanted us to fail. In addition, the "choice initiative" in District Four became very political because kids were being permitted to apply to any school. It was because of the "choice' program that MCSM was created in the first place, but jealous officials downtown attempted to destroy us.

When I arrived at Brooklyn headquarters, I was immediately harassed and questioned about my current position. I was actually told that I didn't exist in the system. They claimed that they could not find my name in the personnel listing at Manhattan Center and, therefore, I would be shipped back to the Bronx, as there were no openings for me to fill at MCSM. My instinct was correct. When I explained to this bureaucrat who was making these personnel decisions, that, in fact, I was the interim acting assistant principal, and needed to hire several more teachers to fill out several subject areas for the fall semester, he lost his cool, cursing me and screaming about the inequities of allowing one singular high school to sidestep the bureau's regulations.

I was beside myself. I know I looked like a fool and weakling when tears started to run down my face, but fortunately, a four-foot-tall, elderly secretary who overheard the commotion suddenly came out of her office to console me and excuse her boss for his behavior. She told me to go and get a cup of coffee and, by the time I returned, the situation would be resolved. I really did not know what she meant by being "resolved," but I left the office to catch my breath. My thoughts returned once again to *flipping burgers*, as I doubted the ability of this lovely woman to exact anything positive for me from this arrogant man. I was wrong.

After the longest coffee break of my life, I returned to hear the words, "I took care of everything and you should return to MCSM." I wanted to kiss her!

I returned to school still shaken but confident that I would now be safe to spend my career participating in this wonderful experiment.

It was a long and stressful summer. Little did I know what awaited me when I returned in the fall.

Chapter 7 – A Whole New Culture

For many of us at Manhattan Center, life during the first few years resembled Camelot. The close-knit family atmosphere shared by a small faculty and student population provided us with a most unique set of circumstances. With a pupil enrollment surpassing one thousand students, a relatively small number for most New York City high schools, many of us knew the names of every youngster. The collaboration among faculty to foster positive growth and nurturing and our outreach to kids to decrease anonymity appeared to be working to everyone's advantage.

I came into this job knowing full well that although I was beginning another year in the profession, I still considered myself a novice as an administrator. I believed that there was tremendous room for me to grow professionally, especially because these teenagers came to school with new issues on a daily basis. One more challenge presented itself when we learned that the principal who had originally hired me left suddenly in the middle of the summer. Totally caught by surprise, our staff was unprepared for the new school year, not knowing what agenda or vision would be presented by our new leader. In less than four years since our inception, there had been so many supervisory changes. Many of us were very worried that an already fragile organization might now be toppled.

The end of August arrived, and it was apparent that a new principal would bring new changes to the school. Hopefully, this person would be a no-nonsense person who prided herself on academics and professionalism. Within the next few months, all of our programs were looked at carefully and every staff member was evaluated. All budgetary items were reviewed for their cost-effectiveness. Initially, there was tremendous nervousness by the staff because for the past four years the school had built upon its successes, and the comfort level was established with the previous administration. However, it became clearer to me each day that there was much in the way we did business that needed to be changed.

As I began to look at the school community with a larger lens, I felt that there were some areas that needed to be addressed. From my own observation there were a number of staff members who seemed to be very weak as teachers. They were chosen early on to teach at Manhattan Center because of their great reputation in their previous school. For three years I tried to understand why they were considered "stars" but just couldn't determine why they were not performing well. Perhaps they were getting lazy or suffering from burnout. I did feel that several faculty members were prima donnas, and were very territorial in their classrooms. As enrollment increased, the need to share facilities with all three schools in the building became even more urgent and instructors no longer enjoyed the luxury of having their own rooms. Improving academic scholarship was certainly a priority. The new principal wanted to make the school even better and did institute badly needed changes. I was totally on board, and we hit it off from day one.

Many of us were concerned about our positions since some of the licensing requirements had been questioned. Once we would be looked at as a regular traditional high school by the central board and possibly lose our special status as a collaborative with the local district, we could forfeit our jobs. We were afraid that if a new person would clean house, our responsibilities at the school would be in jeopardy. As a result, acting assistant principals, teachers, school aides, and paraprofessionals who were missing the proper licensing requirements for their positions were asked to get their papers in order and obtain appropriate certifications. My own credentials for the assistant principalship to which I was assigned were rightfully being questioned. After all, I was supervising three different subject areas, and certainly was not licensed in all three. As a result, the superintendent paid me an unexpected visit. He was cordial and supportive but did put me on notice. I was given one full year to prove myself. In that year, I had to become fully licensed as a high school assistant principal for Foreign Languages or I would be history.

Although I was duly certified by New York State, in order to remain at the school I would have to pass the special licensing exam of the NYC Board of Examiners. The problem was that the exam had been frozen for over five years because of some rumored controversies connected to the questions. Since the test had not been given in quite a while, my status as an acting supervisor was justified and could not be questioned. Yet, at any time, a more senior person holding the city license could replace me. During those five years, I worked as an administrator without the pay of a supervisor. Maybe the real motive to freeze the test was simply to save money. Can you imagine working as a CEO and being paid as an executive assistant? Nevertheless, I accepted my position with dignity. However, I had no recourse and hoped that, in the end, I would receive my due salary and be fully licensed.

Finally, the certification test was revived and offered later in the year to applicants such as myself. It took one full year to be scored. In that time, I earned enough licenses and degrees to wallpaper my office! I had become licensed as a high school principal and assistant principal in several areas, certified both by the State and the City of New York. Several years later, the Board of Examiners was dissolved. This dual licensing requirement of asking educators to become certified by the City and by the State with two separate tests had always been very unfair and problematic.

Aside from obtaining the required certifications, I was expected to boost academic results, which was a major priority of the administration. In the interim, I had to hope that a more senior assistant principal would not *bump* me out in the days to come. There were a few close calls, but I managed to stay put until I became fully licensed and officially appointed. Of course, then I had to worry about becoming tenured, and not getting kicked in the ass by someone in the city more senior while I stayed afloat during this probationary period.

Meanwhile, I decided to get involved in numerous projects in the hopes of making a good impression and at the same time familiarize myself with everything in the building. Several components of the school's mission and vision were extremely favorable to my own growth and success as a teacher and administrator in this East Harlem high school. For one, I was personally driven to make sure that these impoverished youngsters from the *ghetto* had the opportunity to be competitive with middle-class suburban kids. At least my principal allowed me to become empowered as I accepted responsibilities outside of my subject area expertise.

This was no easy task. As a specialized math and science high school being housed in a building built before World War II, it became immediately apparent that our resources were sorely lacking. Once again, the understanding that we lived on the *have not* side of the *have* and *have not* hemisphere jolted us into the sudden realization that our school was insufficiently wired to accommodate internet access. Our computers were not networked to run a computer on the third floor, which allowed for the work to be printed on the same level. Rather, the student had to run down to the library on the first floor to pick up the paperwork he was creating on his computer. Our technology was seriously antiquated. How absurd!

Once again, the dedication and out-of-the-box thinking of the staff came into play. With the help of AT&T, who provided the wires (not the workers to do the actual wiring), my staff and I drilled holes in the floors and ran the wires from end to end of each floor, walking between the walls to make sure the wires followed completely until everything was connected. I can't forget those days of kids and staff trying to untangle hundreds of wires for every device, as well as the daily struggles to unjam the pinhole paper getting stuck in the printers. God bless the world of wi-fi.

While this was going on, I was informed that a boa constrictor, which was supposed to be resting in an aquarium in one of the elementary school classrooms housed in our building, had escaped. So, while we were rewiring the computers, we were asked to look out for the escapee, while walking between the walls. Can you imagine how paranoid we all were at the thought of coming face to face with a boa constrictor? Unfortunately, Boa was never found.

At the end of the day, we were able to get our kids onto the worldwide web through an amateurish, but adequate, method of rewiring. Our technology classrooms were so archaic. In fact, I remember bringing in twenty coffee cans to place on the outlets on the floors because the kids kept tripping over them, causing power failures. Years later, in the late '90s, we became part of the Manhattan Empowerment Zone for internet access. Until that time, we had to make do with the little we had.

You know that saying about "all work and no play?" Well, we decided that the kids needed to have the opportunity to expand their worldview beyond their neighborhoods.

The administration, including my fellow assistant principals, were all on board with providing a host of experiences for our students. Ski trips were arranged along with museum outings and theater parties. Over twenty varsity athletic teams were created, and mentoring collaboratives were established with General Electric, Mt. Sinai Hospital, Columbia University, and NYU. With only a five-year history, our reputation as a safe school, as one that strove for academic excellence, and one with a college-bound program for all, was being noticed citywide. As a result, volunteers in private industry including IBM, Hewlett-Packard, NBC, and AT&T reached out to invest their resources with us. Neighboring community support groups and local businesses and universities followed suit by offering students opportunities in art, entertainment, science, mathematics, and technology. In fact, our partnership with the Repertory Dance Company of East Harlem put us on the map with other prestigious music and dance programs. These public/private partnerships made the difference between what our budget could buy and what we could actually offer to our students to broaden their world.

Miraculously, our school population also consisted of multitalented students who would eventually make a name for themselves in entertainment and the arts. Rappers, singers, and film and music executives along with actors from the Harlem area attended Manhattan Center. These students added character to the school community and, although their academic interests were not in math, science, or technology, they were driven to succeed through the support and care of the staff and administration.

These were special kids. One very famous rapper by the name of Mase (five No. 1 singles on the U.S. Rap chart) loved my daughter, who was a young kid at the time. She was a fan of his and was probably the only white kid in Rockland County who had photos of this African American entertainer taped to her wall. One day, as a favor to me, he called her at home. She refused to believe it was him until he started rapping. What a kick!

Another rapper, Cam'ron, who is still popular today, was a sweetheart. Every time he saw my wife at the school, he would literally lift her off the floor with the biggest hug. When he graduated with his master's degree, my wife happened to be in my office when he arrived to show me his diploma. He said to my wife, "You always told me not to use negative influences as an excuse to fail, but rather as a reason to succeed, and that's what I did." This guy was so caring. I remember escorting the kids on a trip to Niagara Falls. My family joined us, and my shy four-year-old was entertained and embraced by Cam'ron as he showed her how to sport her Care Bears boombox on her shoulders just like the high schoolers.

Chaperoning the annual Senior Prom and monthly school dances were at the top of my list of volunteer activities. The kids kept me young. They taught me how to dance, I learned their lingo, and after a while, even my own family couldn't understand me. When I started to walk and strut like the kids, my family almost had me committed. I was truly having the time of my life!

Chapter 8 – What We Do for Love

Not everything was so rosy! As we began to approach an enrollment of 1,500 kids at Manhattan Center, it was crystal clear that we would, like most other inner-city schools, come upon our fair share of very needy kids. We would be naive to think that every child accepted into our school would be problem-free. The word *needy* is used very loosely since all teens are needy in one way or another. Yet, we encountered many extreme situations of child abuse, sexual abuse, neglect, abandonment, poverty, and crime beyond anyone's wildest imaginations.

We can debate whether or not it was our responsibility to intervene to address these unfortunate situations, but for so many of us caring educators, we were left with little choice. Our resources in the guidance, social service, and mental health areas were very scarce, so we needed to be creative and very dedicated to the cause.

These kids were ours. As with any issue, not everyone was on board, and the level of dedication did vary dramatically from teacher to teacher. We may have all been given the designation of *mandatory reporters* but not all of us believed we were *mandatory doers*. Moreover, forty years later, I am still asking why there are still so many people in our society who want to punish the children for being poor, for living in a downtrodden neighborhood, for being born into a dysfunctional family unit, or for being victims of abuse.

Historically, kids coming from lousy neighborhoods went to lousy schools, which resulted in lousy outcomes. Can you imagine if doctors said that they would only treat *well* patients? Similarly, there are teachers who only want to teach perfect kids. Manhattan Center was created to revolutionize the way we admit students into high school, so that kids would not be punished by being forced to attend schools with bad reputations. Here we are many years later, and the verdict is still out about how schools should develop admissions criteria to best serve diverse communities.

A case in point was Maria, a feisty East Harlem resident with a fighting spirit to succeed. Living only a few blocks from the school, Maria's life experience covered the gamut of challenges: being raised by a working single parent, sibling rivalry, dysfunctionality, and incredible poverty. Maria was struggling to find her identity within the school culture. Her sensitivity to racism, whether generated by fellow students or teachers; her rebellious response to teachers' demands; and her disagreement with anything that was mandated by school authorities made her a frequent visitor to my office. I listened and gave her the attention she needed. However, hating to admit it, I found her criticisms of certain staff valid, reflective of someone who cared deeply about her education. Yet, her reactions were destructive. In her attempt to make the point, she was cutting classes, being disrespectful to her teachers, and failing to abide by the regulations set forth by the administration. Her stubborn nature was contributing to her downward slide and, with college around the corner, we needed to act fast to turn her around.

Fortunately, we had a team of caretakers who truly believed that this kid could succeed. She was sharp enough to recognize which teachers were not a good fit for Manhattan Center. Several of us, however, being more sensitive than others, spent endless hours together after school, providing tutoring, mentoring, and guidance sessions. We created a strategy so that she might pass her courses and apply to several colleges. Yet, we also knew that unless we took her out of her environment, our academic plan would never work.

Several colleagues offered to take her home temporarily, but we knew that such a move would not be wise given the guidelines and mandates to which employees had to follow. However, one former staff member who had left the school several years ago continued to maintain contact with the student and agreed to allow Maria to spend the balance of the school year in her home. With the help of these surrogate parents and continued oversight by the caretakers, Maria is today a professor and an accomplished author with a family of her own, who continues to pay it forward in her university and in her community.

Maria kept in touch over the years and never hesitates to describe the love she felt for me and the other staff members who made her believe in herself. The love was mutual. Certainly the family who managed to get her through these very difficult chapters in her life deserves many of the accolades.

Maria represents thousands of students who passed through the doors of Manhattan Center and, because of some very dedicated and loving staff members, were able to follow in her footsteps. So many of our educators are the hidden figures behind student success.

Certain kids really do stand out in your mind, even twenty years later. Let us refer to this next student as *Student J.* This young lady was a very soft-spoken, obedient kid. From day one, her charm and thirst for knowledge were apparent to the entire staff. Perhaps, her very quiet nature often separated her from the crowd of loud, boisterous, opinionated teenagers who represented the majority of the student body. Year after year, her grades and scholarship were indicative of someone who would go far if luck and opportunity would go her way.

We were fortunate enough to be located near Mt. Sinai Hospital, with whom we established a collaborative program called the Mt. Sinai Scholars. Mt. Sinai Hospital would provide the support and resources to high school students who showed interest and potential to enter the field of medicine. Students in this program who maintained a very high GPA were placed in a Bridge to Medicine program with the hospital. Those who continued to show promise were offered a four-year medical school program with financial tuition assistance. *Student J* became a Mt. Sinai Scholar.

We heard very little from her during her years at Manhattan Center, her focus being on her academics, and we knew even less about her home life. The one thing we did know was that each and every day for four years, she was escorted to and from school by her father, who spent the hours in between sitting in the library, reading voraciously. Manhattan Center was truly a home away from home, not only for *Student J* but also for her father.

We all assumed that her father was the overprotective sort, especially since our school was located in a pretty sketchy, gang-ridden part of Manhattan. Years later, after *Student J* graduated from one of the most prestigious schools in the country, we learned that she and her father were homeless and that the cafeteria and library were the safest places for dad to hang out while his daughter was in school. Today, *Student J* is a practicing physician in a major city.

To the credit of the tens of thousands of teachers across this nation who do God's work on a daily basis, educating all of our children, regardless of race, ethnicity, religion, or zip code, we do it out of love, not monetary compensation. Our working conditions in inner-city schools are abominable, with deteriorating buildings, asbestos-filled walls and ceilings, rat and roach infestations, and next to zero supplies and resources. And yet, we teach...

Chapter 9 – The Beat Goes On

The years began to fly and Manhattan Center, thankfully, was no longer the best-kept secret. Our leader was highly skilled at building the school's reputation and our name was recognized. We became more polished, had earned much acclaim in the district, and were proud to have put together a great team of administrators in each subject department, along with guidance and supervisory staff overseeing discipline, budget, and the entire building plant. We were all held accountable and pushed to do the best job possible in accomplishing our mission. We continued to stand by our so-called claim to fame, as a nontraditional neighborhood high school.

Unlicensed personnel were in most cases transferred. Staffing was now computerized and linked to the district and to the superintendent's offices in Manhattan, certifying that we were, indeed, a "real high school," with few traces remaining of the original collaborative between District Four and the High School Division.

Other than the priority given to the middle school students housed in our building, we were now completely divorced from the oversight of the decentralized district in East Harlem.

We continued to attract kids from neighborhoods all over the city. Our school became synonymous with college prep, partnerships with private industry, and, above all, safety.

The youngsters were wonderful, for the most part. To be honest, we did experience our share of suspensions, discipline problems, cutting classes, and academic failure. Nevertheless, since 1982 our school had grown, had become synonymous with excellence, and had built a program of which we were proud. Close to 90 percent of our kids were accepted into colleges, with great financial aid and scholarship packages. For students and staff, the new norm based on the past few years was looked at as survival of the fittest. Teachers who had lived up to the challenge, and kids who met our academic demands, were able to persevere.

We parted ways with those teachers who could not or would not live up to the task of working with inner-city students with the forward-looking goal of attending college. The 20 percent of the student body who could not handle the academics or attend classes on a regular basis were encouraged to leave once all supportive measures were exhausted. We had a small percentage of kids who could not handle the rigor of a math, science, and technology program. In an attempt to prevent them from becoming dropouts we decided to place them in much smaller schools with personnel that provided more guidance and intervention. Many transferred out, while others just trailed behind for five years until they graduated. A very small number actually did drop out. Eventually, the Department of Education sent out a mandate that we could no longer transfer our students who did not seem to be a good fit. Whichever freshmen arrived as ninth-graders would remain with us, for better or worse.

For me, personally, *the beat really did go on*. I was taught how best to evaluate teacher effectiveness and write observations that would withstand scrutiny. In addition, because we were still a small school with an extremely limited budget, I was tasked with the responsibility of overseeing three departments, which normally would be assigned to three separate supervisors. In the long run, however, it was to my benefit. I was asked to take on many programs and collaboratives, emcee graduation each year, and be present for activities that were not part of my job description.

Supervising three departments and being involved in so many activities forced me to have a thorough understanding of my job, her job, his job, and their job. When asked a question by a student regarding any of the three departments under my charge, or any other matter, for the most part, I never had to say, "It's not my job." Further, if the question was, in fact, outside of my purview, I knew exactly where to send this youngster for an answer. This engendered great trust from the student body, and later proved to be a major asset in my career.

I attended PTA meetings, which most supervisors did not care to do. I staffed the MCSM booth at college fairs and, as previously mentioned, made commencement exercises my own.

I also taught and supervised students in a college prep leadership program with New York University called Project Must (Mentoring Urban Students for Teaching) to prepare our youngsters for a career in teaching. This joint program with NYU was so incredibly important to me as I became acutely aware that the future of the teaching profession was in serious jeopardy.

Even today, attracting good candidates into the profession is most difficult. The salaries in large cities have improved substantially, but working conditions and additional responsibilities placed on teachers have discouraged many folks. Educators are now asked to include in their lesson plans topics on bullying, gender identification, HIV, racial tolerance, sex education, substance abuse, suicide prevention, and conflict resolution. There is little time left for teaching content in the subject area. In many smaller districts across the country the problems facing the inner-city kids may not exist in their suburban surroundings, but salaries are kept very low.

Under the supervision of NYU professors in the doctoral program, our high school students mentored youngsters in the middle and elementary schools. It was an extremely exciting experience. Moreover, our students received college credit from NYU with guaranteed acceptance into the school if they maintained a ninety or above average through their senior year. For me, personally, teaching in this program was truly exciting. Escorting the kids to NYU's campus each month was a special treat. It worked wonders for the student body and even boosted my own self-esteem.

The tradition of seeking out public/private partnerships continued. NYU's Project Must, along with the GE Scholars Program with NBC Universal, IBM's Mentoring Program with Columbia University, and the Mt. Sinai Scholars Medical Programs for future physicians increased not only the public face of the school but the level of respect directed at our students and teachers. MCSM was a unicorn in the midst of East Harlem. The current principal made this networking a major priority, and certainly served as a great role model for me professionally.

I was extremely comfortable in my job as assistant principal when, during the summer of 1995, I received a phone call while traveling through Vancouver, British Columbia. The call was to inform me that our principal was leaving unexpectedly and that I would be designated as her replacement, making me interim acting principal until a permanent candidate would officially be selected. At first, I thought it was a hoax or a misinterpretation of the original phone message taken by my daughter. I was in a state of shock. Why me?

Including myself, there were four assistant principals in our school who held principal's licenses by both New York City and New York State, all extremely qualified and capable of growing into the job.

When I arrived home, the outgoing principal and superintendent asked to meet with me to make it official and offer an explanation as to their decision to place me in this position. They indicated that they were certain that they were leaving the school in the best hands while also cautioning me about the possibility that I might not be the ultimate choice as a permanent replacement. In my mind, acknowledging that the East Harlem community was highly populated with Latino and African American residents, I realized that preference might be given to a minority candidate. I swallowed hard and got a real knot in my stomach. Here we go again!

It took me a while to defrost, and, soon enough, I realized that I had just inherited a huge responsibility with the daily reminder of the typical saying "the buck stops here."

In taking on this challenge of a lifetime, I knew that at that moment I could be starting from square one, which seemed to happen to me many times in my career.

Chapter 10 – The New and Improved MCSM

So, what would go through your mind if you suddenly found out that you are now responsible for three thousand kids and two hundred staff members? Sheer panic and sleepless nights set in knowing all too well that the residents and shopkeepers of our East Harlem community depended upon the climate of our school to help them survive in their neighborhood. They looked to the educational leaders as they would to the guidance of church leaders.

Our Manhattan Center campus also housed a preschool, elementary school, and middle school in addition to the high school. I was held totally accountable for the workings of the entire building and all of its constituents. To say I was questioning my decision to accept this position was an understatement. As an interim acting principal, I was not entitled to a pay raise. At that time, under the existing union contract, no additional monies were assigned to supervisors in an acting capacity.

So, after spending five years as an acting supervisor earning the very same salary (or in some cases less) as the teachers I supervised, I was now going to be paid on an assistant principal's line while working as a temporary principal, with all of the additional headaches and responsibilities that it entailed. (Years later, the union forced the enactment of legislation to pay acting supervisors the same salary as those who had been formally appointed.) For me, the timing of getting a raise commensurate with the responsibilities of the job always seemed to be off. In addition, the notion that I was merely a caretaker of the position until someone more competent, more experienced, or more political was appointed kept me very vigilant. So, my mantra became "failure cannot be an option." I would go down fighting.

As I began informing friends and colleagues of this life-altering promotion, the comments I received included "sink or swim," "it's lonely at the top," "you must be nuts," or "you can make more as a teacher without the headaches." Not very encouraging, would you say?

During the summer I decided to reach out to active members of our UFT union to inform them that I would be taking over for the principal and looked forward to working with them and the rank and file to move the school in a positive direction. I knew that if I could get union representation on my side, my life at MCSM would be substantially easier. The response to my calls was not always positive, and at times I felt as if I were receiving condolences. I do not recall being congratulated by everyone but was happy to hear a refreshing welcome from most of the faculty.

It was apparent that the first blow to my ego came long before the first day of school.

However, I soon realized that my reputation was based on previous incidents of disagreement when I was assistant principal of several subject area departments. It seemed that there was some *bad blood* that did not go away. The failure rate for a number of teachers was high, and in the estimation of some instructors, they were not at fault. The same response always pointed to the inability of inner-city kids to learn. During those years I wasn't the sole decision-maker in the school, and so I was limited in what I was able to do to effect change. At the time I had no choice but to accept what I considered to be mediocrity, and deal with the situation at a later time. I also had to accept the fact that the union position was to protect its members, and they were doing their job in representing them. For many years I was a member of this union myself and called upon them for assistance. They had to be respected and appreciated.

In hindsight, these conversations very early on in my supervisory career actually gave me the beginnings of my to-do list. Improving the failure rate in all content areas would be my first priority. Whether my interim acting position lasted one year, and I would be gone, or I would prove everyone wrong and be permanently appointed, it was my obligation to make the youngsters in my care my main concern. If failure wasn't an option for me, then it shouldn't be an option for the students.

The former principal handed over a great school to me. On an academic level we had experienced tremendous improvement in scholarship. However, I saw things from a different perspective and soon realized that for me there was a serious disconnect. Although the attendance and graduation rates exceeded those of many other high schools, there was an unacceptably high failure rate in some subject areas, especially those that required passing grades on New York State Regents exams. How could that be correct? Sifting through the data, I realized that many of the kids were repeating classes in night school and summer school, often taking the same class two or three times. These facts were hiding in plain sight. Yet, the same routine continued year after year.

The graduation rate always remained high because the students made sure to make up their credits in time, but this practice still did not sit well with me. With this understanding in hand, I put the second item on my to-do list. I was determined to lessen the enrollment rate for night and summer school repeater classes by getting kids to be more attentive to their academics. Easier said than done!

Typically, when a new hire takes on a position, there is support staff around to guide him or her through those initial confusing days. Unfortunately for me, my former principal had left the school, the superintendent who placed me in this acting position had just retired, the district school board on the high school level was virtually unknown to me, and neither the chancellor nor his deputy knew me from a hole in the wall.

I spent July and August of that summer making numerous visits to the school to observe the summer program. I met with staff and visited the high school district office. I made hundreds of phone calls to inform my teachers and administrative team of my new position. I took notes furiously from each conversation, determined to open the doors in September with a decent budget, challenging academic programs, a good student enrollment, and a vision of improving academic results.

Fortunately, I had been a fixture at MCSM for twelve years and was reasonably involved in many facets of the school environment. The students knew me very well, and because I had actually supervised three departments as an assistant principal, many of the teachers knew about my work ethic and sincerity regarding academic scholarship. Inasmuch as I made numerous attempts at promoting interdisciplinary curricula with other content areas, I knew every teacher in the school. Nonetheless, the changeover from directly supervising the teaching team as an assistant principal to becoming their supervisor as the school principal created a relationship problem with some of the faculty. When issues become personal, opinions change.

My mother's words kept going through my mind. She would say, "Wisdom will prevail, and common sense will guide you."

I hoped that would be true...

Chapter 11 – A Seat at the Table

These past twenty-three years in education have been filled with numerous successes, some failures, many changes, and an abundance of *flavor of the month* endeavors. This notion has not changed. If we come back in the year 2050 teachers will still be reinventing themselves and recirculating the same old trends under a new name as the decision-makers change. I laugh when I communicate with friends and family currently working in the schools who report the same nonsense that I experienced when I first started teaching.

My lifelong dream was to become a principal. I knew that if I ever had the chance to make things better in pursuit of a common goal, I had to use the experiences working with my predecessors as a path to better approaches in education, creating a school community rather than a school building. Realistically, though, I knew I would make my own mistakes. I only hoped they would be small ones.

And so, I began my untenured tenure as an interim acting principal.

I started by conducting a *blitz*. During the next several months, I observed every class and met with one hundred teachers, paraprofessionals, and teacher aides from the high school. I then met with another one hundred staff members housed in my building, including security personnel and a large custodial and maintenance crew. The teachers from the elementary and middle schools in our facility met with me as well, making numerous requests. Even though these two small schools had their own directors, I was designated as the overall guy in charge of the entire building. They were hoping that I would comply by giving their faculty all the resources and services that they were unable to acquire previously.

Sharing all the rooms and facilities with two other schools was a great challenge that most other principals didn't have to face at that time. Years later it became quite common in many large buildings to create several smaller schools and dismantle large programs of three to five thousand kids. These meetings and subsequent encounters with everyone in our school were truly informative and very gratifying. Yet, not everyone was happy when I could not always say yes to their demands.

The good, the bad, and the very ugly began to surface. My first instinct was to take on the most problematic issues and add them to my already burgeoning to-do list. Knowing that really nothing could be ignored, everything became a priority in my frenetic day.

The biggest stumbling block to improving academic performance was change. I did not want to antagonize the union delegation and did try to work with them by using the powerful art of negotiation. So, as the failure rates continued to climb, nothing significant was accomplished to my satisfaction. Small fires were extinguished, and failure rates went up and down from year to year without much happening to truly raise the bar in a systemic way.

I did not want to put the blame on the teachers, but I did want to make it our responsibility to reverse the trend once and for all.

In an attempt to become more familiar with the high school-mandated state curricula, I made the unusual request of requiring course outlines from the staff in the mathematics and science departments. It became apparent that many teachers in these subject areas, as well as those teaching history and English, were not on the same page. They were teaching completely different content. For instance, students in one American history class might spend two days, six weeks, or no time at all on the essence of the Constitution, while students in other history classes might not even take up the topic, depending on the *teacher's* comfort level with the subject matter. From one instructor to another there was absolutely no consistency with the topics they were teaching. Yet, all four hundred students studying American history had to pass the same Regents exit exam in June. No wonder the failure rate often reached 60 percent departmentwide. This number was an average since fortunately, we did have several teachers who did extremely well with their kids.

Many folks held their position by saying, "We are professionals. Don't tell us what to teach, or how much time to spend on each topic, or which curricula to use." In my attempt to intervene, I was concerned that several teachers might hit me with a grievance as a means to voice their objection.

I was never going to accept such mediocrity in the way we deliver instruction, and I certainly felt that it was my responsibility to hold all of us accountable for results. Yet, I was not so naive as to believe that a top-down mandate would work, either. So, from that point on, everyone was going to have a seat at the table. The teachers were correct in their quest to make their own curriculum decisions, but minimally they should be consistent department wide. Having been a product of the schools in New York as a student, and having taught in the schools for many years, we were always required to follow a standardized course of study common to all teachers with minimal essentials of learning for all. These decisions were based on compromise, while following the state guidelines at the same time.

I knew when I accepted this position that I would be fighting for my own survival and, at the same time, fighting for what I had believed in for many years, which was that *ALL KIDS* deserved the same quality of education. Inasmuch as they all had to pass the same exit exams, they should have all been taught the same content, the same curricula, and the same course of study within the same school.

Realistically, I knew that I could not clone my best teachers. Each educator had his/her own strengths and weaknesses; each possessed a unique level of creativity that no one intended to question. Minimally, though, each of the approximately four hundred students taking the same subject should have followed the same course of study and/or calendar of lessons regardless of instructor. If the differing levels of academic performance from class to class was a factor in the amount of time necessary to complete a topic, then adjustments could be made in terms of enrichment or remediation.

Nevertheless, the consistency needed across the same subject area became a non-negotiable item. No longer would I accept a comment like, "They don't need to study the Constitution since it was covered in junior high school." Regardless of our personal opinions regarding the NY State Regents exams or which topics the state examiners chose to include or exclude on the test, we had to prepare our kids on this particular assessment. The state called the shots. Passing these tests was a graduation requirement. If we felt that other topics should be included in the curricula, we could offer elective courses not required for graduation, but ones that would broaden learning.

This agenda of mine would prove to be a tough fight. How would I be able to enforce this mandate when several instructors threatened to file grievances? There seemed to be a fine line between what I felt was my duty to improve instruction and the claim that workplace rules in the UFT contract prohibited the issuance of any mandate such as the implementation of curriculum.

I was desperate to lift the graduation results. I was intent on promoting a four-year high school plan rather than the five or six years it was taking for some of our students to graduate. I decided to hold emergency meetings on a voluntary basis with my supportive teachers and the "stars" in each department. Those with stellar Regents exam results were totally onboard. These same educators began twisting arms, inviting their colleagues to rewrite the calendars of lessons within the framework handed down by the State. It was no longer a top-down mandate from me, but one recommended by the stronger instructors who were respected for their academic track record.

Without dictating what to teach or how to teach, worthwhile and useful professional development sessions were arranged by the teachers. I gave them carte blanche to hire outside experts, if needed, without the worry of the cost factor. This change was seen as an emergency and the funds needed would be secured at a later date. Fortunately, there were many talented and expert educators housed right in our building, and the cost was nothing.

I was blessed with great people. The few folks who opposed my views did try to sabotage everything I did and made numerous efforts to intimidate my supporters. It was not uncommon for individual staff members to try to change the beliefs of those instructors who supported these collaborative curriculum changes. This attitude was rare in our school but was conveyed to me on occasion. I hear this notion repeatedly from many teachers in many schools throughout the city. It was quite prevalent in my last school in the Bronx.

For most, getting a seat at the table, having a voice, having someone listen to them, for a change, was the best approach to moving this effort forward. Most instructors started to realize that they couldn't expect different results by doing things the same way, year after year. For ten years, all I heard were the same excuses with most of the blame being placed on the kids, on their parents, on the State curriculum, and on the administration. Finally, the light bulb was turned on, and we began looking at our own practices to spearhead much needed change.

As an assistant principal with twelve years of experience, I used to bang my head against the wall, noting that some teachers had achieved a 90 percent passing rate on the Regents exam, while their colleagues could only muster a 30 to 40 percent rate of passing. This poor record of scholarship went on year after year. My hands had been tied previously when I sought to question the results and hold these same folks accountable. This culture drove me crazy! Now I wanted to give my best shot at sharing best practices in a systemic way with the leaders in the pack who were consistently successful.

When you need surgery, you look for a surgeon with a great rating. When you need a lawyer, you look for one with a winning history. Why do we not search for the best educators for our children? Why do we continue to cast blame on everyone and not choose to look at our own classroom practices? Since all our classes were heterogeneous, for the most part we had the same students with the same abilities and expected similar success.

Every school should function as a "teaching hospital" where the best and most experienced train others and share in the responsibility for overall scholarship. At this juncture in my short time as principal, I knew I was dreaming, but this goal became my reach.

To be perfectly honest, we never got teacher training right. Without dwelling on the hundred-year-old criticism of teacher preparation courses being led by academics who have never stepped foot into an inner-city public school, who teach theory and philosophy of education rather than the reality of it all, our educational leadership in preparing folks for this tough job must change course. Early on in the university student's concentration in education, the instructor should partner with local school districts, providing internship opportunities, apprenticeships, and field work as a means to better expose future candidates to the job. What better way for a school district to recruit strong teachers than to be able to evaluate them early on in their college career? On the district-wide and citywide level, we would be better served by diverting the thousands of dollars spent on hearings for U-rated teachers to creating teacher mentors and support staff in the schools.

In any case, I was hoping that we were on the road to recovery. At MCSM, we had a captive audience. The kids were selected to enter the ninth-grade class from a large pool of applicants. Yet, we were still looking at a recurring passing rate of 50 to 60 percent across the board. At times we did see a sudden blip, but it was not consistent. This annoying trend was totally unacceptable.

The union and I met frequently to iron out our differences, and we truly wanted to work in harmony. The only thing that worried me was the thought of not getting my official appointment as principal at the end of the school year. I was finally making headway with the staff and I really didn't want to end my run. I was on a mission to move to a minimum of a 90 percent pass rate in all subject areas, regardless of the number of enemies I'd make along the way. It was worth a shot.

So, I began working fifteen-hour days, seven days a week, chipping away at the resistance, one teacher at a time, in a logical, cordial, and encouraging way. I might lose the war, but I wasn't going to lose this curriculum battle. Again, the staff knew me well, having seen me teach and supervise programs at the school for twelve years. In most cases, mutual respect and dedication characterized our relationship, and the teachers knew how I felt about accepting mediocrity. It was time to dig deep and aim high.

Everyone had a seat at the table. Everyone had my home phone numbers and everyone enjoyed my open-door policy, with unlimited coffee, tea, or hot chocolate, whenever they needed to have a conversation or a refresher moment. No appointment was necessary. Suddenly, my office was filled with teachers as early as 6:30 who wanted to discuss their craft or their issues, or just needed some tools to ensure success. I was beginning to need a larger table and more seats. We were becoming a much more collaborative staff.

Chapter 12 – Surprise, Surprise!

The fight was far from over, and not everyone was onboard with the curriculum rewriting project. I really should correct myself in saying "rewrite," since I discovered that many of my colleagues had never created a written course of study, known as a course outline, nor did they use an approved city or state curriculum guide. These educators believed in the notion of *winging it*. Others, however, continually revised, updated, and prepared a detailed daily plan and/or weekly set of lessons. This observation brings me to the belief that this profession is notorious for paying too many teachers to wing it, paying them as high-priced babysitters, while others devote hours preparing at home. Welcome to the world of civil service, where everyone receives the same salary, irrespective of performance. Perhaps the one-size-fits-all notion works for clothing, but not for education.

Nevertheless, rather than preach to the converted, I put this assignment in the hands of the individual department teachers, who proceeded to take charge and revamp the current disjointed plans, which sorely needed to be standardized. Fortunately, they were able to convince each other of the academic value of having this very worthwhile tool in each subject area toolbox. Moreover, contrary to the belief of some faculty members, they were able to convince each other that, in the long run, having these standardized plans would make life easier.

For me as an administrator, the best gift of all was the fact that, at last, they would hold each other accountable for integrating the course of study and for the results of the final exams. I only wished that those teachers who moved on could have seen the true spirit of collaboration that evolved. For many instructors working together on a daily basis was new for them, and in certain content areas it was a first in the twelve years of my tenure at the school. In fact, a good number of teachers began to arrive earlier than usual to attend curriculum writing meetings and did an incredible job in motivating the naysayers to get on board.

Those opposed often gave everyone the *evil eye* for working overtime without pay, but no one seemed to be intimidated or threatened by these actions. I guess the time had finally arrived when most teachers themselves truly wanted this standardization as a means to hold each other accountable. Each department wanted to have a real workable product to continually modify and adjust in preparation for the exit exams in June.

I was ecstatic! This was a win, not so much for me as for the kids. Now all the students in each subject area, regardless of the teacher in front of the room, would receive the same educational package. Years ago, the curriculum folks at the Ed Dept. used to call this guide "minimal essentials." The value-added benefit to this newly acquired package was the ability to present new teachers with an outline and set of learning objectives for every course they would be assigned to teach. For inexperienced instructors these materials were invaluable. In the past, new people were told to "wing it" or figure it out for themselves. In addition, this guide was a gift to substitute teachers who stepped into an already difficult situation. My wife has done substitute service in our community. She continues to be amazed that at some schools she receives absolutely nothing from absent teachers, while in other places she is left with a huge package of materials and instructions. This responsibility should be basic. Some things just don't change.

I had moved the needle in terms of standardization of curricula, but this action was only the first step. The next step was to move the academic results in a northerly direction. This goal was heavily dependent on the effectiveness of the teaching staff. Would they deliver? With each curriculum guide was a set of objectives that needed to be met and a set of measuring tools to ensure that student learning was taking place.

Of course, overshadowing all of these concerns was the question of my permanent appointment. If I didn't succeed in getting that official placement as the principal of Manhattan Center, I would lose the confidence of my beloved staff as well as the momentum created by this effort.

Chapter 13 – A Leopard Doesn't Change Its Spots

Courses come and go. Lesson planning for some instructors rarely changes. Department exams get adjusted from year to year. Yet, you can be sure that the teachers who fail over 50 percent of their students on a regular basis will continue to do so, regardless of all the support and assistance in the world. There are some exceptions, but in general you are either, as I have often said, "into it" or not, and the blame game continues. What a great way to make a living, earning a full-time salary while making excuses for the lousy results. These educators were in denial.

Yet, this time around the sentiment in the school seemed to be somewhat different. It was the department staff in many content areas who were beginning to hold each other accountable. Instead of the pressure just coming from me, teachers began to take a collective interest in wanting their colleagues to have greater scholarship. If some looked bad, they all looked bad.

For many, the sharing of best practices became contagious, and the stellar instructors offered to model their strategies, time management techniques, and classroom routines on a regular basis. In fact, to their delight, I gave up those annoying monthly faculty conferences for true staff development. Even though this mandated contractual hour held after the regular school day, only once a month still seemed like an inconvenience to many. Now teachers were on their own to choose how they wanted to spend the time. Volunteers in each subject area created a list of topics of interest and circulated sign-up sheets before each monthly meeting. The idea of teacher volunteers leading a faculty conference was revolutionary. This practice was much more productive than me lecturing them about district and city mandates, which only created a *gotcha* culture. Yet, very little could help the unpopular, ineffective, low-performing teacher who just didn't feel a part of a data-driven group of educators. It was time to plan my next step.

Of course, union regulations prevented me from removing those teachers who were tenured. Little information was on file from previous schools documenting their poor academic results. Generally, their very mediocre performance included an extensive history of disciplinary problems with their students, resulting in low attendance. In many cases these folks were not brought to task regarding their lousy track record. Little was put in writing when it came to their instructional practices other than an occasional observation report of one lesson a year.

Other than convincing these teachers that they would continue to feel out of place in a data-driven environment or trying to persuade them to transfer to another school, what was I to do? I began a mentoring program and encouraged them to seek help from their colleagues. For some, working in a collaborative environment was not a good fit and another school would have been better. In most cases, they were reluctant to ask for assistance and often ran to the union to complain. I was often faced with a grievance. The teachers had the right to grieve, and it was the job of the union to represent them. Again, I had to respect that law in the contract.

The chapter leaders and I worked well together, and we did try very hard to work out issues favorably and establish compromise. Each grievance required me to leave the school building to attend three separate hearings, taking so much time away from my day. The truth was, I really didn't want to transfer these teachers and allow them to influence other kids in other schools, which many principals tended to do as a solution. Instead, I preferred to help them all I could, but in cases where they posed a danger to children I had to try to remove them from the classroom. These severe cases were rare, especially when the instructors were truly beyond help. They really needed to consider life in a different profession. After all, becoming licensed as a teacher is never a guarantee of success or suitability. Not everyone is cut out to work with teenagers.

In either case, this was a monumental task, and extremely time-consuming, debilitating, and overwhelming. On the other hand, it was time to stop passing these underperforming teachers around the district. Just because we were in an inner-city school did not have to mean that we become a dumping ground for those educators who could not succeed elsewhere.

New York City has had a long tradition of placing the worst teachers in the poorest neighborhoods, giving way to a self-fulfilling prophecy. It became a vicious cycle of pumping out generation after generation of children receiving a subpar education, often leading to an increased dropout rate. Worse than this assessment was the persistent knowledge that New York City had once again succeeded in resegregating many school districts based on the family's economic status, which had an impact on the number of qualified teachers being attracted to certain schools.

I refused to allow Manhattan Center to become a safe haven for underachieving teachers. I made up my mind that I would just have to document everything and anything that was damaging to kids, and if I had to attend hearings then that is exactly what I would agree to do. It was not pleasant, but the students came first. I only wish that administrators would take the documentation aspect of their job more seriously. In conversations with many teachers today in schools in New York, Florida, Massachusetts, North Carolina, and California I am told that they have not been observed in their classrooms for years. Parents of kids in these schools complain that when they report a problem to the principal they are told that nothing has been documented regarding these poor-performing instructors. I fear that this issue continues to be prevalent throughout the country.

Would this move jeopardize my permanent appointment? Was I going to rock the boat just a bit too much? It did not matter. I was moving forward. I took the risk and ended up spending countless days in Brooklyn at the hearing office. It is not easy to describe my experience with grievances without breaking down into tears. After driving two hours to the hearing office, the lawyers often did not show up. They loved to delay these scheduled sessions and stall, as long as possible, while Rome was burning. They tried to wear me down in the hopes that I would remove the negative letter or evaluation. What a waste of my precious time! When they did show up, the meetings were delayed even more.

Finally, when we sat down to discuss the letter that I gave the teacher for his/her personnel file, the lawyers often called me names, accused me of lying, and most often brought up other unrelated issues. After hashing out every single word in my documents, they tried to twist my arm to remove the letters from the file. If there were multiple letters, they tried to negotiate a deal. Once again, I refused, since any negotiation would simply mean that the teacher in question would only return to the school and resume influencing the kids with the same negative practices for another few years.

This entire process was so degrading and so insulting to my position as an instructional leader. This demeaning process had to stop. There was absolutely no discussion when you enter a classroom and see students running around the room or sleeping on their desks and the teacher is oblivious to the lack of discipline or respect. Case is closed! There is nothing to negotiate. We would not put up with this treatment toward our own children, so why should we tolerate it for the kids we teach? The children deserved better.

Sadly, this issue of poor discipline and poor classroom management continues to be prevalent in schools with a weak administration and in places where the culture of the organization sets a low bar for respect and academic scholarship. We continue to walk into classes where kids are swinging from the chandeliers while in other rooms you could see, feel, hear, smell, and taste a true learning environment.

Chapter 14 − Lonely at the Top

My first year as principal was a rude awakening, as predicted. Some days it was business as usual, fulfilling the typical duties of an administrator, greeting kids, observing teachers, addressing parents, attending meetings, being threatened by the bureaucrats. However, on numerous occasions, I was challenged by truly unanticipated events.

Apparently, based on State audits of statistics submitted by previous administrators, there were a number of high schools in NYC, including MCSM, that were cited as having "ghost classes." This citing was based on the number of no-show students who had not been removed from the school's register and were still being considered present and eligible for per capita school aid.

Of course, I knew nothing about this practice, and was not even certain that the finding for our school was legitimate. The fact that these accusations were on the front cover of all of the local newspapers and heard on major television networks sent me into a panic. Soon enough, the edict from the higher-ups was to remediate the issue by re-programming the entire school in the middle of the semester. What a nightmare! Besides the total confusion and chaos created by having to change student and teacher programs, I knew my budget would be cut once these *ghosts* were dropped from my total population. The damage for MCSM did not come close to what occurred in other schools with much larger populations. The larger the school the easier it was to create classes that did not really exist. For us, fortunately it came down to a loss of three classes, which we were able to consolidate into other subject areas without having to transfer teachers. It could have been devastating, but the experience did serve as a good lesson to be very vigilant in the future.

That citing wasn't all. Soon thereafter, I received an unannounced visit by State education auditors who were interested in my Special Education and Bilingual programs. Due to the complicated rules and regulations set forth by the State, it was determined that my class sizes were out of compliance. This decision resulted in the reduction of the number of classes, the increase in the number of students per class, and in the transfer of staff to other schools. The remaining teachers were called upon to take on additional burdens to adjust for the loss in personnel.

"The buck stops here," as I have been told many times, became synonymous with my title whether or not I was responsible for the situation at hand. Yes, it was very lonely at the top. As interim acting principal, I figured my days were numbered after these two incidents. I was not tenured and there was no one to defend me.

When everyone went home, I stayed behind to pick up the shattered pieces of what were excellent programs. I was leaving my office after 9:00 in the evening on many days, contemplating what other problems would reveal themselves. My staff was extremely supportive, offering me frequent doses of compliments or condolences, as the situation required. The stress, however, was becoming unbearable.

It did not take long for the next test of my mettle to smack me in the face. Soon after the incidents with the State auditors, a student entered my office to tell me that a staff member had acted "inappropriately." I will not provide the details, but my reaction was one of horror. My workshop training in sexual harassment kicked in. I had a really bad feeling about the ramifications of this accusation. Having seen MCSM in the media after the *ghost classes* fiasco, I knew it was only a matter of time before the press would grab hold of this story, too. How right I was!

As required, I immediately filed a report with the Office of Special Investigations, which would look into the allegations against the teacher. In addition, I had to inform my supervisors on the district and central levels. Of course, I was hoping that none of these accusations would end up being true. Before I could hang up the phone, I saw the TV cameras, news reporters, and neighborhood residents staking out their places in front of the school, trying to interview the kids. How did this story leak so quickly? Columnists from the local papers even slept out in front of the building to get to the victim upon arriving at the school. It was sickening trying to fend off these hungry journalists looking to vilify the NYC public schools and their principals. Sadly, these incidents did occur from time to time, and dealing with the press only made matters worse, because they questioned the students and photographed them without permission from their parents.

The next six months became an absolute nightmare for all concerned, including the victim and for me, as I became the target of attacks by the students and parents, not because of my behavior, but because of the disruption to the school. Nevertheless, I truly felt horrible for the youngster, who became traumatized by the incident. Unfortunately, that was just the beginning. In years to come there were accusations made against other personnel in the building. Most often they were not true, but I was still required to file a report and wait for instructions from an investigative team.

Eventually the situation calmed down, and we started to put out other fires. We worked in an environment of fear and heard about ongoing investigations in many schools on a daily basis. Our public institutions seem to thrive on scandals.

Months later another issue cropped up that dealt with a citywide finding that there were employees who were working as volunteers. This practice was of course permissible and encouraged, but many were found to be working without being fingerprinted. I was not quite clear about this finding, but I immediately became alarmed because there were so many people participating in volunteer mentoring collaboratives in all three schools housed in our building. We often had guest speakers as well. Did this ruling apply to them? Were hundreds of volunteers in my school working without being fingerprinted? I feared that I would be out of compliance with central headquarter regulations once again. It didn't matter that I was not the administrator who hired these outside resource people, some of whom had been part of the MCSM family for years. These folks were now under my charge. Another aha moment!

From that time onward, every single adult who stepped foot into the building would have to be fingerprinted if they spent time with the kids without the presence of a regular licensed staff member. I knew that this endeavor would be costly and time-consuming, but I refused to have to deal with this issue again. The best advice that I could give any supervisor is to protect the kids and "cover your ass." Every single participant in my afterschool programs and collaboratives, be they mentors, tutors, or volunteers working with students, would have to go for training and be fingerprinted. In the process of having this effort completed, I did discover that most of my mentors had previously complied with the mandate.

It sure was getting lonelier at the top! Well, at least I was given a *pass.* I did receive a warning regarding a number of frequent visitors to the school who did not have the training, and of course, became paranoid thinking that this finding would hurt my chances of getting a permanent appointment. It turns out that as soon as other school principals heard about this situation, they too realized that their schools also had numerous volunteers who were never fingerprinted. I did everyone a major favor by sharing the procedures involved, and coincidentally, shortly thereafter, a chancellor's memorandum was issued outlining this hardly known regulation. News traveled fast!

Chapter 15 – A Seat at the Table – Part Two

How do you define loneliness? Following the grueling experience with this teacher who acted inappropriately, which lingered for months because the press wouldn't let it go, I found myself steeped in self-reflection, sadness, grief, and disappointment. Although my very supportive staff offered kind words, compassion, and even their sympathies, their comments about me "getting the big bucks," which I wasn't, and not wanting to touch my job "with a ten-foot pole" added to my feelings of loneliness. I needed to work through this crisis and my frequent anxiety attacks on my own. As always, I turned to the kids.

I loved these children. At times I found myself hugging the kids even though school regulations were clear about not showing this type of affection. After all, the students were of high school age and problems could arise. These youngsters needed the nurturing as much as I did. So many of them never received this type of attention at home. I needed a *student fix*, so I called upon the senior class teacher advisor, who was also the coordinator of student affairs (COSA), to arrange morning meetings with different teams of kids. My thought was that in order to stay on top of student issues and gain credibility with the student body, I had to empower them. If I could accomplish this feat, everyone would then have a seat at the table. For my own sanity, I had to be with kids who always made me feel better. I wasn't sure, however, that an invitation to a 7:00 morning meeting would be appealing to them, as classes didn't begin until 8:35. Boy, was I wrong!

With additional effort, we were able to recruit ninth-graders who would have their seat at the table for four years. They were flattered to be sitting side by side with seniors, who helped to build their self-esteem and teach them the ropes (not always the best ropes, though). Believe it or not, there were days when I had standing room only, with over fifty kids showing up to my office, which was meant to hold twenty people maximum. Often, we had to move to the library. Initially, I wasn't sure whether they were coming just for the donuts and coffee or if they truly wanted to be part of a student-based decision-making body. Moreover, since our organization was not a neighborhood school, kids needing to arrive at 7:00 from other boroughs had to leave home in the dark, often before 6:00. The early hour and lengthy trip to the school didn't stop them from piling into the building.

It was probably the most rewarding part of my day. The kids prepared an agenda of student concerns, with the promise of not allowing the meeting to turn into a gripe session. I had my own agenda of student issues, as well as positive updates and upcoming events and projects. We all compromised on the time allotted to discuss each item. As the news of the group having a genuine voice at the table got around, more and more students attended. The icing on the cake came from curious teachers who decided to frequent our sessions as well. Many folks were willing to put in the extra time beyond their contractual responsibilities.

I could not let the refusal of others to join us ruffle my feathers. I was able to start my day on a positive and refreshing note, setting aside all the negativism that plagued the system as well as the people who continually tried to sabotage this beautiful effort. My eyes get all watery thinking about the love that we shared with these kids each day. The growth and maturity demonstrated by these youngsters in all the grades were phenomenal. They began to feel comfortable in their own skin. Timid kids became outgoing leaders, and their report card results began to soar as soon as the school started to mean so much more to them. The students had a purpose. I, in turn, was ecstatic. I was even more motivated now to create additional student choice opportunities and experiences through projects, clubs, and collaborations. It was exhilarating!

Some of the kids were still not convinced that their seat at the table would mean much. We immediately had to put their suggestions into action, so that other youngsters in the building would see that someone was actually listening and considering them as equal partners. Within days we created a school recycling program with volunteers from each grade overseeing the project. The students even engaged the middle and elementary school children housed in our facility. Next, the seniors scheduled voter registration drives and signed up almost the entire class. Before long, we had clean-up crews and "Graffiti Gorillas" for school beautification, blood drives, child care services, charity drives, and student-run groups working with parents at events such as new school orientation, high school fairs, and holiday celebrations. Our youngsters created the school's

National Honor Society, and even those youngsters who did not have the high scholastic grades to be accepted as members were willing to partner with the club officers to offer community service. In addition, our student leaders represented our organization on every citywide event publicized in the newspapers such as New York City Cares, the New York Marathon, and Penny Harvest.

As the number of student-endorsed and student-initiated activities increased, I tried my best to participate in some with the little time left in my day. I did work with the cleanup crew washing tables in the cafeteria, replacing toilet tissue in the bathrooms, and scrubbing down desks. The kids needed to see me get my hands dirty. After all, I wanted to be a good role model. The school's intercom and loudspeaker system became my favorite toy. Each morning I announced to the entire student body the new initiatives as living proof that there truly were seats at the table. At times I did abuse the loudspeaker. After all, on the day that Frank Sinatra died, and the entire city was lit up in blue, I promised the older staff members that I would sing "My Way." The kids thought I was losing my mind, but at least we stayed connected.

The youngsters put our name on the map, and college recruiters were already knocking on our doors to meet their future activists. Again, we needed a much bigger table. My heart was bursting with pride, and I was no longer feeling that lonely at all. By the way, our girls varsity basketball team took first place citywide, and I was called upon to accept the trophy on their behalf at Madison Square Garden. At least this time I made it on the major television networks for a good reason.

Chapter 16 – My Day of Reckoning

I truly felt like a foster child in my own school, wondering each day if the *real principal* would walk in and take over. With each new project, collaboration, and initiative to which I put my signature, I had this very uncomfortable feeling that this experience would all be for someone else's benefit. Although I knew in my heart that I was doing it all for the kids, regardless of the outcome, I also knew that in order to fully articulate my vision of boosting academic performance, I needed to continue in this position. Will I be appointed in the end? The situation was becoming more annoying each day, and it started to remind me of that old television show, *To Tell the Truth.* Will the real principal please stand up?

There were fifteen finalists for the position, four of whom currently worked in the school. Yes, this was especially awkward, competing with my own staff members for the job. Yet, we all conducted our business as usual, and for the most part did not allow this dilemma to interfere with our work.

There was one incident in particular, however, that I found completely distasteful. I received a call from the district office mandating me to host a tea for the fifteen applicants for my job and take them on a tour of the school. I thought I was hallucinating! When I explained that it would be unpalatable for me to fulfill that order because I was a candidate myself, and doing the job as the current acting principal, they responded by saying that "it was an order and I had nothing to say in the matter." I had not realized that I was in the military!

Nevertheless, with a lump in my throat and a hole in my heart, I arranged the tea for my competition. I took them on a tour of my school, answered a million questions from the applicants, and described the programs that I had created while serving in the position. There was tremendous interest on the part of the applicants. Miraculously, but curiously, no one questioned my own interest in the job. It was a bit weird. Perhaps they were simply showing respect and thought I wasn't in contention. This event was one for the books! In any case, I lived through this nightmarish day and waited to receive the schedule of the "C30"— One, Two, and Three Level interviews—which is the formal process used by the High School Division to select a principal.

The following day, I tried to put this insanity behind me. I couldn't help but think that I had given away classified information about the school to my enemies. This feeling intensified when I unexpectedly began receiving strange calls and unexplained written letters from my staff expressing regrets that I would not be appointed to the position. Where did this rumor come from? Did they know something I didn't know?

Apparently, after investigating the origins of the messages, it became clear that someone had, indeed, started this rumor, perhaps one of the applicants for my position. Over the course of the next few days, I was inundated with similar sympathetic messages. Without a formal interview ever having taken place, why were there faculty members engaging in such behavior? After all, the supervisors in the school who were also applying for the principalship continued to act very professionally during this entire year, even supporting me in doing the job to the best of my ability. They cared more about the kids than their own career interests and certainly did not want to be disruptive or partisan. To this day, I still appreciate my colleagues for being such consummate professionals and good sports.

This was an awkward situation for me to be in, and I wondered what would happen with the other administrators who were contenders if I did get the job. If they were to leave, end of story. However, if they chose to stay, would any of them be hell on wheels to deal with as we needed to cross paths on a daily basis? Actually, while working for the Department of Education in NYC, I'd been to hell and back more than a few times, so I was prepared. At least I thought so...

Finally, the date of my first interview arrived. I would face a panel of high school officials, parents, students, and union representation from the school. Since I had been the assistant principal for the History, English, and Foreign Language departments, the delegation had worked with me for a number of years. If I did end up getting the job, I would hope that we would get off to an even better beginning.

I got through the interview and felt I had done well. Yet, until I received the invitation for Level Two (second interview), which would include the superintendent of the High School Division and his team, I couldn't be too sure if they had been pleased with my Level One responses.

Fortunately, weeks later, I was called for round two.

The Level Two interview was somewhat of a disaster. Five minutes before my turn to be called in to face the panel of judges, a good friend and colleague of mine was exiting the room after having had her interview. All I did was simply ask her how she was feeling. In my mind, this exchange had been totally innocent. The contents of her interview were never discussed. With that, I was immediately reprimanded by a member of the interviewing team who thought I was attempting to ascertain the questions. I entered the room shaken and mortified at the accusation. I felt cornered and challenged throughout the entire ordeal. I was too upset to give this panel of judges my best shot. It was doubtful whether the Level Three interview with the chancellor would even happen after this less than stellar performance. Fortunately, I had previously worked with other members of the team who were aware of my passion and track record. I was hoping that they would put in a good word for me and save the day, but I wasn't quite sure.

Weeks passed without a clue. Finally, I did receive a written invitation to the final interview with the chancellor. I had a month to prepare for this day of reckoning. This time, however, I would leave little room for doubt as to who I was and what I was attempting to accomplish as the instructional leader of the school. My strategy was to storm the chancellor's office with the most positive attitude I could muster. The discussion would be less about the questions and more about my achievements. There was one other candidate called to Level Three. I decided that whatever the outcome, I would go down fighting. I was going to knock their socks off.

Coincidentally, the interview was on a Friday evening in May, which was the same evening in which the East Harlem Repertory Dance Company had their yearly concert at my school. Knowing my time was tight, I had the courage to mention to the deputy chancellor that I needed to return to school as quickly as possible to introduce the dance troupe. I knew that this request was a gutsy thing to consider when I was at their mercy. Yet I felt it would be a deliberate way to set the tone of the interview by inserting the fact that I spent many a Friday evening at school, attending dances, basketball games, and schoolwide activities. I was so fired up that I gave them little time to talk. I simply started babbling about the school, the kids, my staff, the parents, and the community with endless passion. They saw me checking my watch several times because I didn't want to be late. They were impressed. I walked out feeling so much better after this interview than after the last one. But, as we all know, anything can happen.

It took several weeks for the decision. On June 26, 1996, I finally received word that it was official and that I would be installed as the third principal of Manhattan Center for Science and Mathematics. My insecure life as interim acting supervisor was over.

My new life as a principal would begin. There would always be a "but," however. This time, receiving tenure as a full-fledged principal would await. The probationary period for tenure as a principal lasted three to five years. I could never seem to get rid of this feeling of being a *temporary*. It would be grueling, but I decided to put that thought aside and revel in my accomplishment. I could not believe I had finally received this news!

Chapter 17 – Promises Fulfilled

The interesting thing about beginning my tenure as the newly appointed principal of MCSM was that virtually nothing really changed. Well, I shouldn't say nothing. My salary went up $5,000, which I considered to be "peanuts" even then. In those days, interim acting personnel were not paid their requisite salary, so I spent an entire year as principal being paid on an assistant principal line. It really did not matter. It was not about the money. I just wanted a chance to make a real difference. The responsibilities of the job were the same, regardless of title or salary structure, and I certainly treated them the same. After all, I was dealing with children whom I adored, and I would not mess up their lives for anything in the world. I praised them as though they were my own and, in many cases, I gave them more attention than my own children at home because they were so needy and neglected.

What did change so dramatically for me was the realization of a wish come true, one that I had been verbalizing about for over twenty-five years. There wasn't a day since 1971 that I hadn't thought about what my life would be like interacting with my colleagues, and how I would handle the job if I were ever put in charge. Realistically, I knew that there would not be any way that I could really anticipate how I would react in any given situation. I can relate this notion to the idea of becoming a parent. I couldn't imagine how life would change or what the reaction would be upon seeing that child for the first time. Now, being this person chosen to oversee a high school, intermediate school, and elementary school all rolled up into one was another story.

I do believe, however, that I completely fulfilled my promise to myself to treat my staff with dignity, respect, and appreciation as my way of saying to them "a job well done" for taking care of these kids on a daily basis. For so many years, both as a principal and as an assistant principal, I was blessed with dedicated professionals who devoted their lives to educating and guiding hundreds of teenagers each day. I never treated this job lightly! Most of my staff had the same set of high expectations and level of dedication, treating the kids as if they were their own flesh and blood.

Their job was 24/7 and I recognized that fact. Only a foolish leader would minimize their efforts. Mutual respect and loyalty are the keys to success, and the positive results coming from this type of organizational culture and work ethic would be limitless. I truly believe that I kept this promise until the day I retired.

Yes, I had my enemies, and not every decision I made yielded the intended results, but hard-working, dedicated educators who did right by the kids most of the time were well rewarded and praised by me both verbally and with written commendations. Most of all, they rewarded themselves with their own sense of satisfaction and self-worth. The naysayers, the folks who couldn't find success on the job or just didn't choose to accept the vision set forth, often left the school. It wasn't always because of their perceived lack of recognition that encouraged them to find another teaching venue. Rather, it was a feeling that they didn't belong, nudged along by their own colleagues, that the MCSM shoe didn't fit them quite right.

We did have several instructors who felt that since we were preparing kids for college, we should be teaching them in a lecture format. Many of their colleagues tried to impress upon them that without interaction, questioning, and debate in their instruction, kids could not learn to think critically. Adolescents need the nurturing and support not usually offered on a college level.

As instructors began to work more collaboratively they began to voice their concern about department teachers who refused to cooperate and get on board. I remember observing a history teacher shouting at another department member, accusing him of destroying the academic results for the rest of them because of his antiquated practices. These underperforming educators began to feel out of place and often knew that it was time to seek greener pastures.

I have to say that this feeling deeply troubled me. I felt as if we were attempting to kick a member of the family out of the house. I did have an emotional attachment to my staff, and I often blamed myself for letting these poor folks down or for failing them. It took a very long time for me to convince myself that I couldn't make a diamond out of a rock. This realization came only after numerous attempts were made to improve teacher performance and multiple resources were put into place, offering weak teachers mentoring programs, UFT remediation workshops, modeling, replication of best practices, etc. So eventually, I was forced to take the recommended path of documenting their actions over a two-year period after nothing more could be done to improve performance. It pained me deeply when I had to conclude with a "U" rating. In some extreme cases, I attempted to transfer the educator to another school, which had a program more suitable to the teacher's skills. Nevertheless, it took a good three years or longer for me to remove the worst cases.

In most professions, eliminating employees who aren't working up to par or who don't fit in with the culture created by the employer and the company team is a simple task. However, in education, it involves negotiating and smoothing things over with the union and the bureaucratic Department of Education. Many teachers who were asked to leave requested to file a grievance with the union. Again, this request was a contractual right. Some grievances resulted in three hearings—the first at the school, the second at the district offices, and the third at the Brooklyn headquarters of the DOE. Often, there was an arbitration hearing, requiring a fourth meeting. On a rare occasion, when a teacher had ten or more negative reports in his/her file, it would require me to attend thirty hearings. Many of these meetings required me to leave the building for four hours at a time.

Nevertheless, unlike other principals, I felt the effort was worthwhile in order to improve the performance of our staff members or those who were detrimental to the growth of the children. Many times, fortunately, issues were resolved and the complaints were dismissed.

I had received comprehensive training in documenting irregularities promulgated by an educator. I maintained clear and consistent records of their actions. Some of the files on these educators were six inches thick! Yet, we had very few in this category next to the number found in many other schools.

Nevertheless, this was probably one of the most unpleasant aspects of my job.

At one point, I received a call from the superintendent's office asking me what was going on in the school because there had been a cluster of transfers. I explained that I was fulfilling my promise to create the best possible child-centered educational facility, which was what I had been hired to do.

At the end of the day the number of weaker teachers who transferred were few, and I received an incredible amount of support from my colleagues. It was like the squeaky wheel making the most noise. I had to remind myself many times over that the majority of the staff members were outstanding and onboard with the vision of the school.

With the understanding that I couldn't win every conflict that came my way with regard to staff judgments, I knew that the bottom line would always be the welfare of the kids. There would need to be, as many have said, "tough love" for students and staff alike.

Chapter 18 – It's Now or Never

Getting the official word of my appointment as principal was welcome news. A year earlier, I would have taken bets that it would never have happened. How naive of me or anyone else to think that my formal appointment would guarantee that everything that went into running a school that worked well would just fall into place! Wrong!

In the coming days, numerous events transpired that were major setbacks for the school, and certainly blemishes on my record. As luck would have it, a State audit was conducted on a number of issues regarding attendance, budget, reading, writing, and mathematics proficiency levels. Many measurement barometers were used in rating a school. I learned a long time ago that many of the tools used to evaluate a school are often skewed, faulty, inaccurate, or inappropriate. Nevertheless, you had to play the game, not offend the evaluators, and tell them just what they wanted to hear. However, when it came to my immediate supervisors, like my High School District superintendent, who preferred not to play any games, I knew that I had to make good on my promise and correct anything and everything the evaluators qualified as "in need of improvement."

To their credit, the entire team at the district office was comprised of extremely competent individuals whose experience and know-how proved to be an asset to me. The team was willing to help out and provide assistance and staff development, if requested. Their level of support was limitless. Wow, what a change from my early days of teaching in the Bronx District, where the major claim to fame from school personnel was the amount of money raised in the bake sale. Top-level employees whom I met in my early days of teaching under "Decentalization" were selected based on cronyism and ethnicity rather than on their track record of improving school performance. Besides, it seemed to me that high schools were held more accountable by central headquarters than middle and elementary schools, which were managed by local boards.

In any case, whether accurate or not, I was not happy with what I was hearing about my beloved school. To add insult to injury, I was hit with the negative reviews while on a Principal's Retreat with my superintendent in Boston. The headlines of the local NYC newspapers read, "NYC High Schools Steal Funding from the Budget with Ghost Classes." My school was cited once again as one of the guilty parties. I was mortified! This accusation had been made once before, and I was positive that the practice was no longer an issue. I knew I was still wet behind the ears with regard to running a school, but I took this charge as a personal affront. I automatically blamed myself even though I had yet to conduct a full investigation. In speaking with more experienced colleagues at the retreat, they explained that many schools were still not removing students who hadn't attended school beyond opening day. "No-shows," as they mentioned, were continuing to be included on school registers as administrators attempted to secure more budgetary funds in the form of teaching units. We were being accused of creating phony classes.

As soon as I returned from Boston, I conducted my own thorough investigation. Fortunately, my assistant principals in charge of budget and student services, along with the programming chairperson, were among the most competent and solidly clean professionals you could find. As it turned out, it was a reporting error, as I had cleared the "no-show registers" by the requisite deadline of November 1. I had learned my lesson from last time when this issue came up. So, MCSM was removed from the *scandal* list. The *gotcha* mentality of the system didn't get me this time, but I knew my day would come. In any case, having my name associated with these false accusations did not help my morale.

In any event, the rest of the negative reporting data from the State was my reality test, and I had to address these deficiencies. I had to be honest with myself. We had a fairly good academic rating since the school's inception in 1982, but if you were to dig deep, you would find a lot of questionable information. The failure rate was extremely high, especially among ninth-graders, and our math and reading scores, although not terrible, were certainly not reflective of an organization with college-bound students taking a very heavy concentration of technology, math, and science courses. In addition, the results on our state writing exams indicated a need for major remediation. Much work needed to be done.

Unlike other mega high schools, which held as many as five thousand students, Manhattan Center was much smaller. Given that our attendance rate was generally around 93 percent, it made sense that we should be able to do a better job academically. True, many of the entering freshmen came to us with a seventh-grade reading or math level, but that was infinitely better than many other NYC schoolchildren. Although we weren't a testing school like Stuyvesant or Bronx Science, our selection process should have brought in more academically focused students, albeit that they were still considered "at risk adolescents." Somehow, we were missing the boat. I began to treat this finding as a real emergency, taking it personally, and vowing to attack the problem as though it were affecting my own children. We, as a staff, had to dig deeper into the problems, aim higher, and find real solutions.

Chapter 19 – The Plan

We cannot minimize the huge accomplishment that was made in producing curriculum revisions, in revamping coursework, and in restructuring calendars of lessons to establish consistent standards for everyone in most subject areas. The staff came together during my first year as their acting leader to change the culture, but it was obvious that more needed to be done to improve our results. The data-driven nature of our school was pointing us in a positive direction for the first time. Achieving a higher passing rate on State exams started to really matter to most people. A few, however, continued to believe that whatever happened was through no fault of their own. More teachers were working collaboratively, with a true desire to improve scholarship.

I felt that I had the staff in the palm of my hand. So, I decided to take the plunge and shoot for a major departure from the way we did business in the past. Our mission and vision for the school did not change, but the practices we put in place to achieve our goals had to be looked at with a different lens. We were not digging deep enough into the issues that continued to be roadblocks to real progress. The notion of expecting different results, while attacking the problems in the same manner over and over again, became more ludicrous each day. This definition of insanity had characterized our practices for too long.

The results of the state proficiency exams in writing, mathematics, and the sciences were shared with the staff. I spent the next few months creating an action team of teachers, parents, administrators, kids, and community leaders. These volunteers were to investigate, analyze, and thoroughly examine the learning and social habits of the kids, both inside and outside of school. We looked closely at the classroom routines and management techniques of teachers, their lesson planning, and testing measurements. Even the parents who gave up their precious time with family and from job responsibilities to be on this new school leadership team had a lot to say. They became extremely helpful in providing some insights into what we might not be seeing in the home, and what issues we needed to address at least with the academics.

The result of many months of discussion helped us to make a really simple diagnosis. We needed to totally revamp the school. We recognized that we programmed kids into oversized classes of thirty-four, with close to two hundred in the gyms, and we assigned five hundred student caseloads to guidance counselors. We used cafeterias and closets as classrooms. Asking for an increased budget was out of the question, as we all knew that inner-city neighborhood schools just did not get the big bucks with which to operate. So, how could we improve the academic outcomes without it costing big money? How much more pressure could be put on my staff, who already worked very long days, with no extra pay? As I said, the diagnosis was simple. The remedy was not.

We came to some important realizations. It was more and more apparent that our ninth- and tenth-graders were not merely deficient in writing and math, but also in the sciences and history. We also agreed that the kids were taking too many courses, the pressure of which was compromising their abilities. Those who had not been challenged in middle school were struggling with the demands of so many high school teachers. In most cases they were not given any homework at all in their previous school, and now they were being asked to read hundreds of pages a night between history and English classes alone.

The time constraints placed on teachers in a forty-five-minute time slot for each subject area cannot be overstated. Imagine setting up a chemistry or biology lab, explaining the procedures and goals of the laboratory experiment, only to have the bell ring while the kids are hanging onto every word. Imagine discussing a juicy novel and the bell rings in the middle of a student's question or comment. Imagine trying to write an essay in half an hour. Imagine having a debate in an American History class and the student is interrupted by the bell before closing arguments. Imagine the frustration of solving half a math problem because forty-five minutes is just not sufficient for a teacher to fully explain the process.

These examples are just the tip of the iceberg when trying to identify the limitations that dedicated teachers and students face each day, while attempting to cover a curriculum thoroughly with a reasonable amount of comprehension. Even today, teachers claim that they do not assign homework because they do not have enough class time to go over it. Math teachers explaining the many steps to solving word problems would need the entire period just to review one example.

Recognizing these situations, we all concluded that, above all else, *TIME* was a key factor in their delivery of instruction and critical in providing students with room for applications and, perhaps, flexibility for the slower learner. Never before had we been able to isolate the cause of a problem that overshadowed so much of the general academic promise. All along, it had been much easier to blame the kids, their parents, their poverty, their neighborhoods, the administration, the Department of Education, the chancellor, etc. Now we had a problem we could address in the hopes of finding a real solution. The question remaining was, "How to pay for the solution?" Our choice was to either buy time or create time without it costing us a dime. There really was only one option. We had to figure out a way to extend the school day or add minutes to subject area classes where the failure rate was the highest.

We had to redirect our thinking, knowing that getting more money would be out of the question. We had to work smarter if we couldn't work harder. Not everything you do as part of the solution needs to cost more money if you are creative with your time. Certainly, mandating anything after school hours would be costly because it would involve security officers as well as teaching personnel who would be paid an hourly rate. As it is, many teachers already volunteered to tutor on their own dime. We were back to the drawing board, and once again, a task force was created. A school leadership team was activated to brainstorm and suggest changes to our CEP (Comprehensive Education Plan), which had to be submitted to the District each year. Was I being too optimistic? Could we possibly be ready with such dramatic program changes by the spring to be put in place by the fall?

I was so fortunate to have many allies who shared my enthusiasm, and were truly committed to change at any cost, creating the time needed to improve academic results. Many staff members, parents, and students joined the numerous committees to come up with a plan. My double personality of being cautious and conservative while also being aggressive, with the ability to think out of the box, became my driver. I knew full well that I was setting myself up for a long fight and much opposition. Even so, I was motivated to pursue this agenda.

Well, I'll fast-forward for now. We did come up with a plan. After many disagreements with those who refused to be convinced of the value of these changes—and after many endless meetings with staff, numerous professional development sessions, many conferences with content area teachers, and several parent workshops at Parent Association sessions—we decided to put the changes to a vote to revamp the traditional eight-period day. According to UFT regulations, we needed a 67 percent yes vote to pass. Our leadership team of staff, parents, and students voted unanimously to approve the changes. The rank and file did vote narrowly in favor. We were off!

The new plan called for ninth- and tenth-graders to be block-programmed for double periods in mathematics, history, and English. Half of the students would take either history or English in the fall, then switch in the spring. The additional time allotted in these three subject areas would enable both teachers and students to engage in unlimited learning opportunities, which would, hopefully, provide much needed academic improvement. The plan was an innovative pilot program, the best part of which was that it would not cost us one dollar more to implement.

I can't minimize my appreciation to the staff for their commitment, planning, and creativity in putting together this project in the interest of their students. This new plan meant that freshman and sophomore grade teachers would have to create a completely different set of lesson plans, calendars of lessons, projects, and exams to accommodate ninety minutes of teaching time. For many, this notion was a great challenge, a real reach for those teachers who were not particularly strong in the classroom or with time management. A ninety-minute class could really be lethal for them with thirty-four kids in the room. So, we decided to solicit volunteers to teach in the blocks, rather than force it upon every teacher in the school.

Since many of the teachers were extremely compatible with other colleagues in terms of work ethic, planning, classroom management, and teaching strategies, they began to come up with creative ways to work together. For example, pairs of teachers in two different subject areas requested to plan an interdisciplinary curriculum. All we had to do was program the same kids back-to-back with both instructors and, voila, you had the makings of a great deal. It was paradise! Instead of forty-five minutes, you had ninety minutes to share, flip-flop, or borrow time for special projects, presentations, and curriculum flexibility for which a traditional forty-five-minute module would never allow.

As an example, a history teacher teaching in a ninety-minute block asked to be programmed back to back with an English teacher also in a ninety-minute block. If both instructors were to have the same students they could actually have three hours of instruction to share. Considering that the American History curriculum included topics that are interdisciplinary with novels and shorts stories read in the English classes, you could create a perfect match. You just had to hope that both teachers could work well together and compromise on how to use the time to benefit the kids. Only instructors who volunteered to pilot this interdisciplinary project would be considered if they wanted to work together.

Team teaching models created learning opportunities that went way beyond our greatest expectations. This model worked like a charm between chemistry teachers and mathematics classes when teachers integrated topics from both subject areas. Instructors who previously shied away from conducting debates or engaging in speaking and writing projects during class time were more willing to take the plunge. This practice became a variation of the block schedule and was implemented upon request. The creative juices were flowing. Today schools across the country are trying to integrate their subject areas in creative ways as long as they do not have to be bound to strict State guidelines in terms of what to teach. Once we remove flexibility from our lesson planning we become more limited in our teaching. Many schools continue to be plagued with having to teach to the test.

This kind of scheduling worked well when we programmed history and English together, mathematics with science, and Foreign Languages with history or English. Interdisciplinary teaching was the perfect method to create what many call "memory pegs" for the kids, especially for students experiencing issues with retention. The more often the content and critical thinking stimuli were mentioned, the greater the chances for recognition and memory recall. Compatible teachers who planned curriculum and taught together contributed to an optimal situation. My only regret was that not every instructor in the school was comfortable enough to take this risk. Obviously, the weaker teachers were intimidated by their colleagues and would never sign up for this challenge, which resulted in such a rewarding experience for all involved.

As a result, the block program was left to a natural evolution. As it gained traction, it morphed into many shapes and sizes with unlimited rewards for both teachers and students. In fact, although it was initially designed for ninth- and tenth-graders, it was later extended to all grade levels in one form or another. Modeling and demonstration of best practices became very common as curious teachers requested to observe the miracles that many of their colleagues were performing in their respective classrooms. Looking back, I realized that I was wise enough to allow this interdisciplinary teaching to be voluntary. Rather than making these changes top-down, it was seen as being totally initiated and promoted by willing and capable staff. I believe that its success and popularity were attributable to the teacher endorsement nature of the project, thereby improving outcomes along the way.

The science teachers, who were particularly frustrated by the limited lab time they were given, requested a similar expanded block program. The failure rate in the sciences, especially for a school claiming to be driven by math and science, was embarrassingly high. More than half of the students couldn't even sit for the Regents exams in science because they couldn't complete the lab requirements. The mandatory completion of thirty hours of lab time to be eligible to take the test, which New York City tried to strictly enforce, sounded good, but no one was giving the schools the time or the money to make this happen. I needed to figure out a way to make this situation better by myself. I needed to think hard and dig deep. How was I going to provide the extra time that science teachers were requesting?

This problem caused many a sleepless night. After all, that is why they paid me the big bucks! At this point, I was working longer hours and enduring more stress than the CEO of a corporation who was making millions and receiving bonuses and stock options. My Christmas bonus was a #2 pencil!

Regardless, I had no right to complain because this job was what I wanted, and I was driven to give these kids a better future. I wanted them to be able to dream beyond their wildest imaginations. I wanted to give them an equivalent slice of the pie that their suburban counterparts received. I owed it to the teachers who shared my passion to do whatever it took to push for greater success. Nevertheless, the thought that always haunted me was that regardless of academic outcomes, regardless of the effort and time dedicated to this job, everyone on the same pay level got the same paycheck. Many states have toyed with the idea of incentive pay, but no one has been able to come up with a plan that truly works. Some districts have provided sign-up bonuses and extra pay to attract teachers with superlative qualifications, but this is never a guarantee or predictor of future performance. The solutions to that problem would be discussed later.

The amount of time needed to enable our youngsters to fulfill their lab requirements and complete their written lab reports in biology, chemistry, earth science, and physics had to come from somewhere in the traditional school day. Although it appeared essential that we extend the day to accomplish this feat, it was crystal clear that there would be no additional funding to make this happen. Realistically speaking, inner-city kids enter high school, for the most part, with huge deficiencies in reading, writing, and mathematics, so even a six and one half-hour school day wasn't nearly enough. I had to find a way to create instructional minutes. My science supervisor was willing to try anything to improve the situation.

I knew that at some point in my tenure I would create enemies with change, so I decided to begin somewhere. The physical education department seemed the likely place because of their students' poor attendance. My teachers were cooperative, but the kids were taking gym classes five days per week, with a 50 percent cutting rate. Since they weren't attending gym for a variety of reasons anyway, it stood to reason that I could use this wasted time by transferring it to the science department. There was only one problem. The State Education Department had a mandate of the minimum instructional time spent in physical education classes in order for kids to receive a diploma. I had to do my homework. Could I steal, borrow, or swap phys. ed. minutes for the science classes?

Although my colleagues and fellow high school principals (there were fifty just in Manhattan) advised me not to pursue this line of thinking because it would generate a red flag for a newly appointed principal, I persevered. I had to make sure that I would not be out of compliance.

After numerous calls to the State Department of Education and numerous meetings with my fellow assistant principals to discuss our options, a little-known secret was revealed to me of which very few administrators were aware. Apparently, it was not the number of days of scheduled gym classes required, but the number of instructional minutes that were mandated. The five periods per week that had been historically scheduled totaled many more minutes, significantly more than the state demanded. I recall very vividly sitting with my assistant principal for administration totaling up these precious minutes on a baby calculator to see if we could pull off this change. Why did no one know this regulation? This newly found gift could provide the extra time for the science lab classes if I made a switch, and we would still be in compliance with the physical education mandate. This change would cost me zero dollars, although it would be very costly with much-expected grief from the gym teachers and the union when they heard I was taking away ninety minutes a week from their time with the kids and giving it over to the lab teachers.

I became an instant hero to the science department faculty and an enemy of the state to the physical education department. The school's programming staff was already at work creating double periods in science for the next school year in order to incorporate ninety-minute labs. The science teachers were thrilled but did present me with an additional "ask." Would I be willing to hire two full-time lab assistants to set up the labs so that they would be freed up to devote the entire lab time to instructional purposes? What a brilliant idea! I juggled the budget around a bit and eventually found the money to hire two lab technicians. I felt as though I had conquered the world! The assistants were able to prepare the labs without the teachers having to waste instructional time in setting up or breaking down the experiments for each class.

The gym teachers, however, were not as thrilled as the science folks. The continuity of teaching only three gym classes per week instead of five was being lost. I had to increase the number of students per gym class exponentially in order to accomplish this tradeoff. The paperwork involved in attendance-taking and report card completion would almost double. I was not trying to be insensitive to the importance these staff members put on their chosen field. Yet, I had to prioritize where the dollars would be strategically spent in order to achieve the greatest advances in academic success. As it turned out, I was able to pay these guys back at a later date. In terms of the kids, I took a gamble. The cutting rate in gym did improve as I had hoped, since the kids only had to attend three times a week.

I weathered all of the objections sent my way by several teachers, and ultimately I won the battle. In a short amount of time, the gym teachers were onboard with these changes, and the science instructors, students, and even the superintendent were extremely pleased. Everyone saw the advantages of this plan. We now had a real chance at moving the needle of academic performance. My original belief that "failure was not an option" was actually taking form, but we did have to dig even deeper to make worthwhile adjustments to the traditional way of delivering instruction.

Chapter 20 – The Psychology
Behind Student Failure

Failure in high school, as previously discussed, breeds a growing culture of negativity. We can compare this notion to a failed diet. So many dieters believe that because they might have temporarily ruined their diet by succumbing to a craving of a slice of chocolate cake, they should permanently ruin it by then eating the entire cake. The damage was already done, so why not forget the whole thing?

I remember kids telling me on report card day that they *only* failed three subjects. I would shiver and mourn privately at such an attitude. However, it was even worse hearing teachers brag that they only failed half the class, though in some cases the results were even more devastating, sometimes reaching a 70 to 80 percent failure rate.

Failure, you see, is contagious when both teachers and students share this negative attitude. It spreads like a disease throughout the school building, in every department, even infecting the security staff who deal with discipline and cutting. With low self-esteem, everyone feels defeated, and the desire to improve is quickly shot down. Student and teacher attendance plummet, cutting increases, and any positive work ethic that remains is dedicated to only the select top 20 percent of the class. The rest are left out in the cold. In plain English, as an organization, we are simply lowering the bar, reducing our standards of excellence, remaining satisfied with less than. Even on an administrative level, assistant principals and principals in other schools would tell me I had no reason to complain about a high failure rate when they were experiencing a much higher rate of failure with their students. How insane!

When we talk about low self-esteem on the part of black and Latino kids, who represented 95 percent of our school population, we have to go back to the source. One doesn't need statistics (though there are many) to prove that when children in impoverished neighborhoods are segregated in schools according to their zip codes, standards of excellence are often absent. Inasmuch as their self-image is set early on, by the time they come to our school, they have already encountered low expectations from their teachers, from their community, and, sadly, even from their parents.

Geography, especially in big cities, often defines the level of education available to the most vulnerable of our youth, those who need our help all the more. It actually becomes a self-fulfilling prophecy. What you expect is often what you get. Furthermore, there was another issue that actually surprised me. Many of our kids of color verbalized to me on numerous occasions that working hard and doing well in school were looked at by their peers as "acting white." It wasn't cool to be smart. Breaking barriers that went this deep was going to be a greater challenge than I expected.

How do you begin to change a culture when such prolonged and systemic failures have become acceptable?

I sought out this job because, having been a teacher, an assistant principal, and now a principal, I was able to see firsthand the innate failures within the many levels of this bureaucratic system. I worked with those dedicated individuals who became teachers because they truly wanted to mold their students into accomplished citizens of this country. Sadly, I have also worked with those folks who considered teaching nothing more than a stepping-stone to a better job or career move, and expected very little from kids. I had been fighting this negative attitude for twelve years while I worked in my last school, with limited success. Now, as the appointed "top banana," I wanted to take on the immense challenge of changing the culture of this school.

I was willing to confront every level of systemic racism even from the public and from the community at large that might subtly contribute to the thinking of a few MCSM staff. As a whole we did raise the bar as an organization in order to make our school the reflection of excellence it was supposed to achieve, but when it came to helping the more difficult students, we often let down our guard. When things got tough the temptation was there to label the kids. We owed it to these children to help them overcome the adversity that they were conditioned to accept without question.

I already knew that I had a large number of hardworking staff members who shared my convictions. They would certainly be onboard. Those who didn't buy in would always be a thorn in my side and I was determined to convert them at any cost. Sadly, many folks did not recognize that they had low expectations and that they demanded very little from the kids. I guess when you are convinced you are not going to get good results, you choose not to even ask for them. I remember several teachers telling me that they did not assign homework because the kids wouldn't do it anyway.

Nevertheless, I was desperate to give these students a better chance at success. As with parents and teachers alike, teenagers become rebellious when they feel that they are being treated unfairly. How we, as a staff, handled these adolescents would also affect school culture and their successes. It was a real tough challenge to deal with a number of adults who felt that "these kids" were uneducable, and furthermore, not deserving of better treatment. This attitude, especially toward minority students, continues to be prevalent in our schools across the country.

I firmly believed that excellence began at the top, and I depended on my administrative staff to deliver and oversee that recipe for success in our new cookbook. I was blessed with a group of assistant principals who, like me, were tired of sugarcoating failure, and had heard every excuse in the book to justify our shortcomings.

When I accepted this job, I was in need of a new assistant principal for the Science department, a new supervisor for English, and replacements for me. When I was given the principalship I had to vacate my position of AP History/Foreign Languages/ESL/Bilingual Education. Little did I know that I would be starting a new job with several retirements that needed prompt replacements. What's amazing when I look back is that I chose three staff members to take over my position when I was doing the job by myself! At first glance, filling these administrative vacancies appeared problematic. In reality, the vacancies created a golden opportunity for me to set the agenda on a positive footing with energetic and creative staff. With one exception, the vacancies were filled with teachers from within who were in possession of assistant principal licenses. We knew each other well. They knew their staffs well. We were all on the same wavelength. I was hopeful.

The results we actually achieved during the years that followed were, in large part, attributable to my assistant principals. All of them were willing to take on teaching assignments during the day and after school and create models of best practices for their colleagues. After all, subject area department heads were selected based on their excellent track record as the instructional experts in their chosen fields. Moreover, those teachers who had participated in building curriculum committees were stakeholders in the success of their students. The success of one became the success of all. These master teachers were willing to provide their colleagues with staff development and assistance with instruction, planning, and classroom management. For the very first time, I was seeing demonstration lessons, team teaching, and sharing of daily calendars and unit tests, the likes of which had never taken place on a regular basis.

The mathematics and science content area leaders were in heaven with the double instructional periods that many of the teachers could now enjoy. The interruption every forty-five minutes by a ringing school bell was a thing of the past, with ninety minutes of instruction allowing for a new reality of goals being met. Only time would tell if these changes would translate into improved scholarship.

Chapter 21 – The Race Is On

There were times when I felt as if I were participating in a race. Was I really competing against someone? The truth was that I was racing against time, as I was still an untenured principal. That feeling of permanency, which I seemed to be lacking, had much to do with my paranoia that the door was always open for someone to replace me and interrupt my plan to take the school over the top. Or, could it be that it was simply the notion that every day that went by in which one of my students failed or didn't live up to our expectations was a day lost in the life of that child? Self-reflection is critical, especially for leaders with tremendous responsibilities and a large number of people to whom he/she is held accountable. Yes, there were numerous hiccups in my first years as principal, and too many challenges posed by supervisors to whom I had to answer. Yet, truthfully, I was the one putting the most pressure on myself.

I had promised the kids and their parents that they would get an education that would be equal to that provided by the wealthy school districts. They were guaranteed that they would be prepared for college. The staff was told that I would be there for them and give them the tools needed to improve academic performance. I also took an oath to myself that all the stereotypes and negative traits attributable to many supervisors or administrators would not apply to me. I knew the kids had to come first but, unless quality of life issues in the working environment involving the entire staff were addressed, the kids would not rise to the occasion.

Finally, I gave my word to community leaders that the school and its surroundings would become a safe haven, especially for residents, shop owners, and local businesses in the neighborhood. I had to convince our partners that we were worthy of their investment. With one of the largest areas of gang activity in the city hanging over us, coupled with tremendous poverty and a very incomplete infrastructure, every aspect of life in East Harlem was a challenge we needed to overcome.

The past thirty years had been dismal for this area, with tremendous corruption, crime, drugs, and despair destroying what was once a thriving place to live, to raise children, and to receive a good education. The immigrants from around the globe who chose to live here presented a beautiful testimony to what community life could offer. Even today you can still observe older residents sitting in front of their buildings protecting their *stoop*, snacking on their ethnic foods, and reminiscing over what they called the "golden years."

Most of this spirit was gone, tainted by the terrible reputation of the neighborhood Benjamin Franklin High School until it was transitioned into the Manhattan Center High School for Science and Mathematics. Obviously, changing the name of the school did not create an instantaneous character change for our organization. By exchanging one name for another, it was simply the appearance of change. The internal changes had to be created by the stakeholders, inside and outside of the physical plant. This huge responsibility weighed heavily on my shoulders.

Our plan was to create a safe harbor that encompassed a ten-square-block area extending from our school on East 116th Street and the FDR Drive all the way to the 116th Street/Lexington Avenue train station. That radius included stores, businesses, churches, and other establishments joining forces to build bridges within the school community. It was a monumental task, made more difficult by the fact that only a third of the student population was from the neighborhood. The rest traveled to school from all parts of the city. The danger of many of our kids being attacked on the subways and buses, or along the long walk from the train station, was all too real. With many parents living far away, the prospect of getting them to become active and participate in schoolwide activities, PTA meetings, and leadership teams appeared dim. Likewise, to call on students and parents to help improve a neighborhood in which they did not reside was also a stretch.

Two huge factors, however, were in my favor. The kids, for the most part, treated school and the surrounding neighborhood as their second home. More importantly, my ability to speak and write in Spanish provided me with carte blanche in this heavily Latino section of the city. My knowledge of Spanish was automatically perceived by visitors as an open invitation to the school, a comfort level to which these families had been unaccustomed. In fact, once I began holding PTA meetings in English and Spanish and communicating with Spanish-speaking families in their own tongue, participation increased dramatically.

My goal was not just to create an inclusive school but to create a school community where everyone was welcome, and our school was theirs. I wanted to give our students the feeling of safety, where shopkeepers and residents would look out for them as though they were part of their own families. I wanted to create an environment where each student would be embraced by the surroundings they chose for their high school education. The notion of fear had to be removed from the minds of my kids so that they could concentrate on their studies and personal growth, keeping their heads up, rather than having to look down. These youngsters had to dream dreams they could never have imagined.

So, when I said "the race was on," it was truly a reflection of my own wildly driven ambition to make MCSM synonymous with success. Honestly, the school had already been pinned to the map from its inception, thanks to the foundation created by my two predecessors. The wonderful reputation it held was testimony to much of the hard work done by those who came before me. Kids were graduating at record numbers. Even more importantly, a greater number of graduates were going on to college. But, for me, it still wasn't good enough. The failure and cutting rates were too high. A significant number of teachers weren't able to bring more than half of their classes to pass the NYS Regents exams on their first try. Everyone could do better. We had to dig much deeper. We needed to aim higher. I felt that we now had the tools and strategies to give the kids and teachers a more complete shot at success.

Chapter 22 – Securing Our Village

When discussing the neighborhood school and the role we, as educators, play in keeping our village secure, we cannot minimize the role of the local police precinct. When the mayor decided to merge the Department of Education's safety and security officers with the New York City Police Department, it was a bold and novel move. After a period of transition during which both forces were sufficiently trained to complement each other, the combination of entities began to work to our advantage.

As an administrator, there was a need on my part to understand the rules of law enforcement that guided the precinct. On the flip side, I felt it necessary to educate the officers with regard to sensitivities and thought processes of adolescents as they related to the mission of our unique school plant. We weren't the old Benjamin Franklin High School, which had been taken over by the city and shut down. We were a college-bound institution, a non-neighborhood school with open enrollment. Of course, kids are kids, regardless, but I wanted my students to be trusted and treated with dignity and respect. There would be no profiling of Manhattan Center children.

The 25th Precinct became a true asset to our kids and proved to us over and over again that our school could not be safe without their assistance. At the same time, the surrounding streets and corridor stretching out to the train station couldn't be secure and thrive unless the high school set the tone in student behavior, which would then contribute to the well-being of residents, storekeepers, parks, churches, and local establishments. All of these elements were intertwined.

Gang activity was plaguing East Harlem. This issue became a serious threat to the safety of our students. Sadly, our challenged Special Education population was most vulnerable, as victims of crime as well as targets of gang membership. All too often, initiation led to sex trafficking and the consequences were irreparable. With the precinct's assistance, we were provided with workshops aimed at recognizing the signs of gang affiliation. We were also brought into meetings with community gang members to better understand their agenda, and what we could all do together to avoid any form of violence, especially as it related to our student body.

Several months ago I attended a conference on sex trafficking, and my discussions with a very prominent prosecutor left me with a frightening feeling. The problem of holding young kids as hostages and abusing them to make money is worse than ever in many of our neighborhoods, and not necessarily in just low-income areas. The offenders don't discriminate in searching for innocent victims, and many of these kids are found around the schools.

Looking back over time, several frightening incidents come to mind. One morning I was informed by a staff member that upon entering the building she saw some older kids in a car pointing machine guns out the window. I was sorry that I had to be the one person who received this alarming news, but I did have to respond in any case. I decided not to call the precinct yet, since I had not seen these kids myself. So, I decided to go outside and have a look. I must have been absolutely crazy to even take such a chance, but my staff expected this protection from me, and I did comply.

I walked out of the school and actually did see the same car pass by once again, confirming what my teacher had told me. Initially, I thought that some neighborhood kids with toy guns were playing a joke on us, so I started to approach them. Fortunately, I finally realized that I would be a sitting duck and that such a move would not be a smart thing to do. I decided that now was the time to put this incident into the hands of those who were really trained to handle this situation. I quickly returned to my office and called the police. Within seconds law enforcement arrived, but by then these kids were gone. I never found out if these troublemakers were real or just playing a game, but you could be sure that my heart did skip a few beats.

The security and the police officers became my allies and were always available to me at the push of a button in times of emergency. My team always had my back literally and figuratively. After late-evening meetings they escorted me out of the building to my car, sometimes giving me a ride on their motorcycles. I was deathly afraid to get on a motorcycle, so perhaps they enjoyed the look of fear on my face as I held on for dear life. The security personnel served on my leadership teams, sat in on my disciplinary and suspension hearings, and always provided me with the latest borough-wide news, especially after school hours, weekends, or holidays when crime would heat up.

Inasmuch as my kids lived in every borough, confrontations that originated in a particular neighborhood would spill over into the school after the weekend or holiday. I was warned. The police officers helped to familiarize me with what they referred to as "street mentality"—an eye-opening concept, for sure. Our students and teachers were always invited to police breakfasts, Police Athletic League activities, and workshops, which provided kids with internships and future career prospects. Some of our students were very interested in forensics and detective work, so our mutual relationship with security personnel was a win-win for everyone.

The idea of treating our children with an "all kids are deserving" mentality was a hard-won issue. Typically, if one of my students was caught with a weapon in the schoolyard or involved in an action that required arrest, they were sometimes handcuffed in full view of our elementary school students sharing the outdoor facilities. This was very frightening, especially to little children. When I asked that the officers take the student to my office without making a scene and cuff him/her there, they agreed. On other occasions, when kids were caught with drugs, they were found lying face down on the dirty school grounds to be searched. Again, I asked that they not search the kids in plain sight and, instead, search them in an isolated area, and they complied once more. We were all about minimizing conflict. With a seat at the table, everyone became partners with the kids' best interests in mind.

There were, however, two incidents of what might be considered police profiling in my nine years as principal that were seared into my mind. On a Saturday morning, I drove to school to pick up four students who were participating in the Citywide Debate Competition. The kids got into my car and, while stopped at a red light, we were greeted by the sound of police sirens. I immediately pulled over and, to my consternation and embarrassment, the kids were asked to exit the car. The police frisked each of my students, assuming that a white driver and four black kids meant that there was a problem. It was so insulting to these kids who were my star debaters with fantastic academic averages and were applying to Ivy League schools, although academic scholarship here was really irrelevant. Not to engage further, I thanked the officers for their protection but was on the phone to the precinct first thing Monday morning. Although our conversations helped us to move forward, nothing could erase this incident from my kids' memories.

On another occasion, in late June, when the kids were sweltering in non-air-conditioned classrooms, a benign incident became a major police action. Feeling edgy and overheated, the kids began to bring water guns to school. That afternoon, while I was away from the building at a meeting, the kids began a water gun fight after lunch in the schoolyard. An anonymous faculty member panicked and called the police, who responded with billy clubs and a paddy wagon.

In seconds, the media was outside filming the chaos. Needless to say, the kids, their parents, and my staff were appalled at what they witnessed. In fact, I actually learned about this incident while watching the news on television from my mother's hospital bed. Here I was sitting with my dying mother feeling terribly distraught, and suddenly I observe my school on all the major networks being invaded by police cars. I left my mother from her bedside in New Jersey and drove seventy miles an hour back into Manhattan to investigate the situation.

The following day, I arranged a forum for all parties involved in an attempt to smooth over the raw feelings in a diplomatic way. Many lessons were learned from this experience, one of which was to make sure no water guns were brought to school in the future. We added this new regulation to our written code of discipline. In addition, more training was needed for my staff in dealing with conflict, and certainly more discussions were required on how to proceed in my absence. It was also time for a refresher forum with parents, kids, staff, and the precinct to review any errors in judgment and restore our faith in this partnership.

In spite of some negative incidents, the overarching feeling between the school and security officers was positive. In fact, as I reflect on the many crises we encountered during my career, the police were there to minimize conflict more often than not. Their intervention in safeguarding our kids during 9/11 and the weeks that followed—as well as during the protests resulting from the Rodney King and O. J. Simpson verdicts, the crisis created by the garbage strike, transit strikes, teacher strikes, asbestos fiasco, hurricanes, blizzards, blackouts, and other catastrophes—was invaluable. Working as a team, we were able to weather the storms that affected us all. With each passing day we became better friends and partners.

I remember relying on security personnel and the police department every time I conducted a fire drill. When the gongs were sounded every one had to evacuate the building and take assigned positions on the streets surrounding the school. The police blocked off the streets from traffic for our safety until the fifteen-minute drill ended. The security team was invaluable in protecting over two thousand kids as they evacuated in an orderly fashion.

Yet there was one situation that required my own personal creativity. Every time we had a drill, many of the kids snuck into the grocery to purchase snacks instead of staying with their teacher. My many threats to refrain from this action did nothing. So I decided to hide in the grocery store ten minutes before the drill only to surprise my darlings when they tried to enter the store. The expression on their face was priceless when they tried to enter, and saw me with my arms folded. I responded with my comment, "Don't even think of coming in here. Get back to your teacher." I had solved another problem. However, the store owner was annoyed with me because he lost tons of business.

Over the years my staff and I volunteered to stay after hours to supervise and chaperone school dances in the evening and of course the annual junior and senior proms. We looked forward to the festivities and welcomed the chance to stay young, and to become deaf with the very loud ethnic music. We learned the dance steps and acquired the rhythm as funny as we looked. Nothing gave these teenagers greater joy or perhaps provoked greater laughter than to see me on the dance floor.

Yet, I have to admit that these activities were often very frightening since we could not anticipate who might show up at the door. We could vouch for the behavior of our kids, but not for their escorts who were not our students, and were often much older. I know we took a chance by allowing guests to attend, and we did end up having incidents with alcohol and some gang activity. Once again, the local precinct and our dedicated school security officers always came to the rescue, providing safety for our chaperones and kids. They danced with the students as well, but always kept an eye wide open. In fact, one of the police officers became our resident DJ. He made sure we always had a blast, but to tell you the truth

I was a bit uneasy whenever I attended an evening event with large gatherings.

There were numerous problems involving the safety of kids that seemed to get better, while others got worse. Now that every kid has a cell phone the teachers have to be more vigilant regarding their use in a school setting. My friend who currently teaches at the school informed me that students abuse their right to have a phone by sexting, texting, and even ordering lunch in the middle of a lesson. The rules for relinquishing the phones during exams have to be very strict for security purposes. Another issue that drove me crazy was trying to plug up all the holes in a huge building where kids had sex. As soon as we closed off one area of danger the kids found another. I hired over thirty school aides just to patrol the halls.

Kids being caught under the influence of alcohol was a problem, but now marijuana has become the new replacement. We never had an issue with cigarettes, but currently "e-cigarettes" are creating problems for teens throughout the country. Once again, all of the situations related to security could have been a million times worse had we not had the incredible support and expertise of our police officers and school safety personnel who educated us on how to do a better job of keeping children and staff safe.

Considering that some police departments across the country are looked at in a very negative way based on the profiling and racial incidents that plague inner-city schools, the need to work very diligently toward improving the relationship between children of color and law enforcement was paramount to maintaining a positive school environment. The local precincts were extremely valuable to us and were often praised for their hard work. When I think about the tragedies in schools in Sandy

Hook, Columbine, and most recently Parkland, my appreciation can't go far enough in thanking my team for putting themselves on the line each day.

Chapter 23 – You Take the Good with the Bad

With all of the monumental changes taking place, it was apparent that the traditional way of delivering educational instruction in our school was gone, hopefully for good. With classes blocked and double periods of daily lessons, the teachers had to reinvent themselves once again, this time in a big way. Their academic planning was completely new and extremely creative. No one could accuse our teachers of using yellowed and frayed lesson plans left over from the Civil War. Though teachers in general tend to be resistant to change, our teachers for the most part were resilient and resourceful when called upon to meet the challenge.

Over the years, the instructional staff had become used to what many called "the flavor of the month" educational plan, which choked them from the top down. I was committed to creating a new reality with improved student-based instruction along with systemic and deeply rooted cultural change. With 80 percent of the staff onboard, the others who disagreed and would not embrace the new plan would follow suit, leave the school, or succeed in killing me. To a certain extent, it became survival of the fittest.

I patiently waited for results on every level. Would double periods and blocked classes really do much to enable kids to do better academically? Would the curriculum planning committees with teachers working collaboratively significantly improve the quality of instruction? Would these strategies, conceived through a figurative bursting of my blood vessels over a repeated pattern of dismal failure, bare fruit? And, yet, the same adage convinced me that I was on the right path... "Don't expect different results if you continue to do things the same way." I know I sound like a *broken record*.

To begin with, most of what we had hoped for was, in fact, being reported. Attendance and cutting were both improving, a function of the double periods, which enabled instructors to keep closer tabs on their students. Moreover, with this new schedule, the individual instructor's caseload of students was actually cut in half, making their administrative tasks more manageable. Subject area teachers were reporting that they were getting more done, completing their tasks, and having more time for applications, which boosted comprehension, especially in mathematics and science. Now that more kids were completing their lab reports, more of them were eligible to sit for the Science Regents exams in June. All of this news was music to my ears. Of course, real academic improvement with improved test scores and a lower failure rate across the board would be the only significant scholastic indicator. Hearing this positive reporting on a daily basis was a great motivator.

When I think back at the hundreds of hours of brainstorming with my leadership team and with committees involved in the task force for reform as outlined in our State Comprehensive Education Plan, I frequently recall their comments and predictions. Teachers, parents, and, especially, the students involved in these planning groups voiced concern about the weaker and less "popular" teachers not being able to handle the new changes. If you ever want an honest evaluation of a teacher's ability, ask the students. They could tell you how many kids were cutting class simply by counting the empty seats. The greater the number of empty seats, the less effective the instructor. Whether by virtue of their weak instructional capability or their disciplinary failures, the less effective teachers were well known.

We did attempt to give the blocked classes over to the stronger teachers, as they could handle a ninety-minute stretch. However, we had little choice when it came to math and science classes, which required an all-hands-on-deck approach, with the entire department involved. We were obviously moving toward a very clear conclusion. The more accomplished teachers got even better with these reform strategies; the weaker teachers, with few exceptions, continued to struggle. These weak links in the chain of our educational reform plan had the potential of sabotaging the entire project.

Furthermore, although the majority of the staff had voted for reform, an interesting phenomenon emerged. A small group of staff could carry enough weight to rock my boat. Regardless, I was not going to compromise my vision nor lower my standards for the two thousand college-bound kids from East Harlem. So, to some instructors I did become the enemy. I had to come up with a plan to help these teachers, knowing full well that it would become uncomfortable. Few people like to be told that they need assistance with their craft.

June arrived soon enough. I waited with bated breath for the results of the Regents exams, report card grades, and, most importantly, the graduation data. I was also anxious about my face-to-face meeting with my superintendent and the one hundred-page tome of documentation for the year that would constitute my evaluation.

The results came in and I was ecstatic! The Regents results showed a 30 percent increase in all subject areas, reaching an 80 percent passing rate, and with some of the stronger teachers boasting a 90 percent passing rate. The failure rate fell to an all-time low for our school. The kids who didn't make the grade would still have to attend summer school. Some teachers documented no failures in their subject classes, although we all knew that standards varied from teacher to teacher. At least with standardized exams, such as the Regents, you were given a more accurate story. The graduation rate stayed constant at over 90 percent. Even so, it reflected a graduation rate for June graduations, rather than including the August summer school repeaters.

The teachers who helped create this new reality celebrated their results and were truly convinced that the double periods and instructional curriculum committees were paying off. Now, I could hardly wait for my face-to-face with my boss.

The day came for my evaluation and, with book in hand (one hundred pages of statistics on attendance, cutting, pass/fail rates, graduation numbers, Regents results, Advanced Placement success levels, math and writing proficiencies, Special Education achievement, suspensions, etc., etc.), I strutted into the superintendent's office like a peacock. His first words to me were, "Which do you want first, the good news or the bad?" My bubble burst in those first few seconds.

I truly respected my boss. This guy was extremely tall, and always impeccably dressed in a blue or dark gray suit. All the principals looked up to him as a true educator. I thought he was brilliant and quite sharp. He was a product of many years of dedication and hard work, and his position was truly earned. Whatever words would be conveyed during our meeting would be taken as credible and constructive. He knew his stuff. Frankly, though, what could he possibly tell me when my data indicated so much success? In fact, only recently, he had asked me to provide professional development to other principals on many of the areas of my evaluation to which we would now address. I was confused. What could be wrong?

I did say his comments were always credible and constructive. While he praised my reform strategies and sprinkled kind words over our improved results year after year, he pointed to persistent failures in that too many kids took the same class two and three times over. So many were still going to summer school. He was absolutely right. There were no excuses. He studied my stats. He dug deep into the most minute details. He wanted me to raise the bar further yet. I respected him for being such an exceptional educator, and for always challenging me to do even better. And, so, I went back to the drawing board, and drafted yet another corrective action plan. This time I had to dig even deeper and aim much higher.

Chapter 24 – A Temporary Defeat

I left the superintendent's office disheartened, to say the least, with my evaluation in hand. My administrative assistant was, and still is, sharp, loving, protective, and extremely tech savvy. She had created the most comprehensive picture of the school's progress I could have hoped for, including impressive graphs, charts, and spreadsheets based on the data I'd provided. Not to be repetitive, but as you know, statistics can be skewed to tell the story you want it to tell. My boss, however, was too smart to gloss over or sugarcoat the numbers that gave an incomplete picture.

We'd been making excuses since 1982. It was now 1997, and we hadn't gotten to the point where *ALL* of our students were graduating after four years rather than five. We had been offering watered-down summer school and night school classes for years. Since night classes were offered in other schools I did not have any idea about their worth or credibility. In addition, we also had been making excuses for the same group of teachers with a consistent track record of failure. We had allowed them to kick the can down the road semester after semester, collecting the very same paycheck as those dedicated to achieving success. We had allowed the cancer to metastasize for far too long throughout the school. It was time to rethink how we dealt with the situation.

It was July, and although I had hoped to tackle the issue immediately, I was obligated to supervise a summer school program for five schools in my district. With two thousand kids repeating classes and August Regents exams on the horizon, I was truly too busy to give my evaluation much thought. Many of these repeaters during the summer were kids from other schools, but there were still too many from my own population. As soon as summer school ended, I took my one-week vacation and, sitting on the beach, ignoring my wife, I began to plan out my next strategy in addressing the superintendent's remediation plan. I continued to try to understand this big disconnect. How could a school with such a great reputation have so many students repeating classes? I was becoming desperate in my search for a real lasting solution.

My toolbox of supplies and brainstorming ideas was running very low.

The one common denominator in addressing issues of failure was, of course, increasing the budget to allow for additional support. Remediation had to include help for unsatisfactorily performing teachers as well as for failing students. The dilemma was that if I moved funds to corrective measures, I would be neglecting those students who wanted to take Advanced Placement courses, additional electives that were not necessarily required for graduation, but necessary to broaden their learning sphere, providing enrichment for college preparation.

To be clear, it wasn't solely my decision. The union and staff had to agree to whatever changes would be considered. The real issue anyway, based on my meeting with the superintendent, was to improve the quality of our instructional programs and teacher practices in hopes of reducing the failure rate and the number of kids repeating the same classes.

The Manhattan High School superintendent's office always received high marks for their expertise in the complexities of educating all children. They walked the walk and talked the talk, making themselves available to help with any issues presented to them by administrative staff. They offered to provide assistance to teachers in need of improvement. Unfortunately, several teachers didn't acknowledge their need for supportive services, nor could they be mandated to accept such services. Furthermore, the union might not agree on the extra time required for these supportive services, as the UFT contract had strict rules on the number of hours in a school day that we could "mandate" for their members. I had to work around this wall.

I decided to begin with the kids. After all, it was really about them. So often you get caught up in the bureaucratic nonsense, conducting endless meetings and spending all too much time on paperwork. I was never one to hide out in my office. I enjoyed chasing kids down the hallways, running after them in the staircases where they might be hiding or creating mischief, patrolling the schoolyards, and surrounding neighborhood streets for delinquents or kids cutting class. The kids knew me well and I knew each and every one by name, even when we reached a level of two thousand students. They often called me by my first name, joked with me, embraced me, gave me a high-five and thumbs-up. I needed to up my game even further. I had to take advantage of our smallness. Yes, for a NYC public high school, our student population was small.

I began to set up an intricate schedule of class visitations—not to observe the instructors, but to preach to the kids. The conversations I had with senior classes, talking about diploma requirements and needed credits for graduation, were very different from the discussions I had with freshmen and sophomores about doing homework, discipline, and attendance. The teachers, for the most part, were very supportive of my visits even though I was taking away some valuable teaching time. Others were in shock, as they were accustomed to working with principals being holed up in their offices. They were surprised that I would take time out of my busy schedule to provide guidance services during class sessions. The usual disgruntled posse felt I was conducting these visits just to look good or hear myself talk. It didn't matter. I owed it to every single student to be a father-like figure, one who truly cared about their well-being and their future.

This new tactic proved monumental. I visited every class and spoke to every student. With much of my work hours being taken up with this effort, my time at home with my family was severely disrupted, with tons of paperwork yet to be completed on my part. To this day, I thank my family for being so supportive while I stepped away to complete hundreds of observation reports. Nevertheless, with such a positive response from the students and staff, I decided to go yet further.

I requested the student transcripts of every one of the four hundred graduating seniors, deciding to meet one-on-one with each of them to review their particular graduation needs. I met with them before school, during lunch, and after school until I covered all of them. I was kind and supportive but had to provide *tough love*. In many cases, I threatened to return prom deposits if attendance didn't improve. Some of the kids doubted my resolve, but by the March report card period, I had returned some thirty prom payments. The kids were incredulous, but knew I had been serious. Rewards came with work, including diligently moving toward graduation.

My actions, though extreme to some, became further endorsed by the city when a mandate was issued indicating that students lacking credits in June could not participate in graduation ceremonies by marching at commencement. No longer was it good enough to graduate in August and be permitted to participate in the ceremony in June. Change was long overdue and everyone was watching to see whether these actions would be enforced. It was perfect timing.

The teachers had my support, and I theirs, gaining respect as a unique administrator to personally monitor transcripts and attendance reports in a determined effort to prevent rewarding those who exhibited negative behaviors. In addition, I maintained an "open-door policy" where teachers were free to enter my office at any time to discuss individual kids and their progress.

It was no longer taken for granted that a senior would automatically go to the prom or march at graduation. These benefits had to be earned.

To be sure, I never liked playing the bad guy. I loved these kids. It was an investment in their future. We began to see the failure, attendance, and cutting rates improve. In the coming years, seniors finally came to understand that these new policies were sacred. Honestly, I didn't get through to every kid. There was a small segment of the school population that couldn't be reached, no matter what was done. These kids were, indeed, troubled and needed greater intervention by guidance specialists. Often, the only realistic answer was to find another school with a better fit or a smaller program that provided entire-day monitoring of the student body. Fortunately, I had very few students in this category, but still felt helpless in not being able to get them to change course. After all, they were my children. I guess I needed to dig even deeper.

Chapter 25 – Assessing the Situation

All in all, I was beginning to feel somewhat accomplished in my mission of changing a fifteen-year-old culture at Manhattan Center. Expectations from the staff and kids were much higher. So much of the nonsense and excuses for poor results were taking a back seat to the positivity wafting through the school building. It is human nature for every teacher, every administrator, and even every parent to say, "I have high expectations." But what does that really mean, and what is our basis of comparison? Yes, the failure rate, attendance, cutting, and graduation rates all showed signs of improvement. The math and science departments showed the most upward movement, credited to the double periods and added instructional time.

History and English classes were somewhat slower to show upward mobility in academic performance for many reasons. To begin with, these subjects didn't have a defined calendar of lessons or curriculum as did math and science. In addition, the teachers themselves weren't as collaborative, as they all had different teaching styles and, perhaps, a more individualistic philosophy of teaching. Having tracked fifteen years of academic results, the highest failure rate in coursework and on Regents exams year after year came from a number of humanities classes. Even when the kids were interviewed and surveyed, they indicated that their most enjoyable subjects were in the sciences.

Yet, there were exceptions, and when you had an inspiring, passionate, and exciting history or English teacher, the kids bragged about their instructor and offered tremendous praise. Thank goodness we had some giants. In many cases the lessons were truly extraordinary in moving their kids to take action with regard to their civic responsibilities and citizenship. They made history come alive and inspired kids to take lessons from our past to improve their lives. Their teaching methods and classroom practices needed to be "bottled" and shared throughout the department. As time passed, I recruited real gems who made great strides and advances in the delivery of instruction. They were able to improve the culture and influence others.

Eventually, we were left with few lacking the creativity and desire to think out of the box and energize the subject matter. Early on, this realization came as a surprise to me, as I assumed that instructors majoring in history chose this subject for their love to debate, question, and think critically. The truth of the matter was that creating relevant and motivating lessons in history required much hard work. Assigning exciting and meaningful projects involved extensive planning, monitoring of progress with each step of research, and a large amount of correcting papers. Many teachers started out with this spark and innovation, but soon became too bogged down with too much work from students in oversized classes. Essay writing, analysis of documents, and critical thinking soon gave way to activities that were easier to manage. At least with blocked classes of ninety minutes, teachers had fewer kids to teach and more time to devote to building writing and speaking skills.

In any case, my goal had to include replicating pockets of talent with mentoring, modeling, and assistance using my more accomplished and patient instructors. When the culture of a school includes a shared responsibility for academic results, that's when you see the dedicated educators helping the others. Unfortunately, there were some veteran teachers who had been teaching for over twenty years, failing their students in large numbers, who could not be moved from their ingrained method of teaching. And so, the cycle continued. On the other hand, some of my veterans were the best teachers and mentors in the school. You cannot generalize, but for those who couldn't change practice, the road ahead was incredibly difficult.

In assessing the overall situation, we concluded that there were many measures that were working. The extra time the students received provided them the opportunity to master the content of their curriculum. Teachers in most subject areas were pleased with their new schedules, allowing them to offer remediation and applications in their coursework to increase student comprehension. Time was a crucial element in increasing learning and understanding. Other elements fell directly at the feet of the teachers. Student discipline, classroom management, and delivery of instruction were the foundations of student learning. Changing these elements would require great introspection. Failure was not an option. Once again, we had to dig deeper into our practices, and set the bar higher, not just for ourselves but for some of our colleagues who were satisfied with their mediocre performance.

Chapter 26 – The Gift of a Lifetime

As the end of June was again approaching, it was business as usual. Closeout activities included grading of exams, preparing for graduation, evaluating teachers, and programming kids for opening day of the summer session. Another two thousand registered summer school students kept me busy. Fortunately, many of these kids were from other schools. Sadly, my school had again been chosen as a summer school site. Although there were four other principals assigned to this summer school location, I was put in charge. That meant that while I was overseeing kids and training attending teachers, the other four principals were guests at the party. If you were lucky enough to be assigned to another school for the summer, you had it relatively easy, but if you were mandated to supervise a large program in your own school the planning for you started early in March. Add that responsibility to the list of inequities in the business of education.

While this craziness was going on, I received an unexpected phone call from the CEO of a community-based organization called the Children's Aid Society, commonly known as CAS. They were requesting an appointment at my earliest convenience to discuss an exciting offer. My initial reaction was more annoyance than interest, as I was as busy as hell with end-of-year tasks. I was more focused on addressing the teachers who disappointed me once again with their failure rate and Regents exam scores. Yet, I was concerned that if I didn't schedule this meeting, the potential offer, whatever it might be, would be gone and forgotten by September.

The purpose of the call was rather strange. My little knowledge of CAS was that they generally set up afterschool recreational programs in elementary schools. I thought that they might be interested in creating a program with the younger kids or early childhood classes housed in my building and needed space for a summer initiative or a project for the fall. I reluctantly agreed to have a sit-down with them. All too often, community-based organizations just call on you to pick your brain or request to use your facilities. I was not hopeful.

Putting this forthcoming meeting out of my mind for the short term, I concentrated on one of the most rewarding activities of my school year. I loved emceeing the graduation ceremony! For the most part, these kids were the first high school graduates in their family. For the parents, it was a day of pride, acknowledging, perhaps for the first time, that their kids finally made it to the finish line. A high school diploma would be hanging on their wall. The icing on the cake was a college acceptance with a significant financial aid and scholarship package attached. This year the graduating class had amassed over $6 million in financial aid and scholarship monies.

It was quite a spectacle! I tried to make my speech funny and something of a tear-jerker, as well. I was experienced in hosting graduations, as I had been doing it since 1987, way before I became a principal. My predecessor assigned this responsibility to me and, over the years, I truly made it my own. So, the yearly experience of "Pomp and Circumstance," with a variety of fired-up speeches, the hugs and kisses as each diploma was awarded, flowers, photographs, and tearful goodbyes all became a highly anticipated annual event. It was now 1998, and each year's graduating class felt special and invigorating. Over the last twenty years I have attended graduation ceremonies for friends and relatives in several parts of the country. The behavior of the graduates in many cases was simply appalling, and sometimes got out of hand. I guess the rehearsals and lectures that I conducted with my seniors days before the event really paid off, since year after year the commencement exercises proved to be a "class act."

With all the excitement of graduation, one thing didn't work out well at all. As anticipated, the students who couldn't march because of the chancellor's new directive had taken effect were heartbroken. We all shared their pain and disappointment. What we didn't realize at the time was that notification of this decision was made at the very last minute. Often, it wasn't until the night before graduation that it was learned that a few students had either failed one or several courses or they had failed the Regents exam. This news made it impossible for them to walk at graduation. This resulted in many families traveling long distances to attend the graduation of a family member who could then not participate in the commencement exercises.

This issue was disturbing and unacceptable, and it became my mission to alert families earlier on about this impending situation. Going forward, I promised to personally scrutinize every transcript and interview every senior at least twice during the year, requiring a parent or guardian to sign off on the meeting notes to make sure they were fully informed. For me, it was a teachable moment. At least, parents in the coming years would be more vigilant early on about the possible consequences of failure and not being able to attend graduation. The familiarity with this regulation did encourage many parents to sit on their kids to study harder and better prepare for exit exams and courses necessary for a diploma.

The excitement of graduation was finally over, and I returned to my office to put the finishing touches on the summer school program, which was to begin on the very first day of July. I could barely catch my breath. Now, my left hand was signing off on numerous end-of-year documents while my right hand was signing off on written protocols for new hires for summer school teaching spots. What chaos and turmoil!

Of course, I kept my appointment with the Children's Aid Society. A very friendly top executive of the organization and a young female member of his staff arrived and immediately began showering me with accolades from community members, especially from our partners at Mt. Sinai Hospital. It was true that MCSM had a very prestigious program with the hospital, called the Mt. Sinai Scholars, through which approximately fifty of our students were being groomed for a fully paid medical school program, but I was shocked that anyone outside of MCSM or Mt. Sinai Hospital would have known about this collaborative. I graciously accepted their compliments but remained curious as to their agenda.

As the conversation ensued, it became clearer to me that this organization wanted nothing from me, but, instead, actually wanted to give my school an incredible gift. When I heard the numbers, to the tune of thousands of dollars over five years, I had a flashback of my childhood, watching Michael Anthony in the television program *The Millionaire* knock on some startled stranger's door with a check for an incredible amount of money donated by billionaire John Beresford Tipton.

Having worked for close to thirty years in the NYC schools, literally begging for pennies to buy supplies, hire staff, and get just the bare essentials to help run an organization, I was skeptical. What was the catch?

My heart started to race, as my typical nervous energy began to kick in, partly from joy, but mostly from the fear of what I would have to do to earn this donation. What hoops would I be required to jump through to receive this award? My experience with grant writing was enough to educate me to the facts that the mandates, site visits, and reporting mechanisms attached to the grant often made it impossible to comply. As it was, my time was stretched to the limit. For me, there were still many unanswered questions.

As the conversation continued, many of my early assumptions were realized. The main purpose of this visit was to create a program to keep the kids off the streets of East Harlem. I agreed that recreational afterschool programs were beneficial to the kids, creating positive experiences, cooperation, and friendships. Being that I already had quite a few varsity sports teams, fully funded by PSAL, which utilized my gym, outdoor field, and small schoolyard to capacity seven days per week, I didn't feel that this offer would fill our needs at the time. However, I didn't want to summarily dismiss their offer, so I tried to drive the discussion in another direction. I needed to be precise in my suggestion of an alternative viewpoint.

Inasmuch as the Children's Aid representatives made it very clear to me that MCSM would be the very first high school to be offered this program, and possibly be a model for any other potential secondary school partnerships that they would envision, I decided to be gutsy and suggest an initiative that would be entirely academic.

It had always been my dream to have an afterschool program where my kids could be safely housed and supervised after school hours and, at the same time, be given that extra learning experience that our budget didn't allow. Currently, I couldn't offer extra remediation for those falling behind, nor could I offer as many Advanced Placement courses as I needed to provide enrichment and college prep. We were always functioning on a bare-bones budget. Our classes were maxed out at thirty-four students. In several cases when we were out of compliance with the state or not meeting their proficiency levels, our instituting corrective measures meant requesting additional funds. The Department of Education didn't think we needed the funding since many other schools were needier, and because we were still functioning well. There were years when I didn't know whether I could safely open the doors in September because my budget, having been severely cut again, did not allow for an adequate number of teachers to run our programs.

With all of this said, I continued to try to sell CAS on the idea of a purely academic program. However, they knew enough about this type of program to voice their concern that I wouldn't be able to encourage a large enough number of students to stay after school for tutoring. After all, most afterschool tutoring programs throughout the city were a waste of time and money, where teachers were paid to supervise empty classrooms. I, myself, had to scrap many tutoring sessions due to lack of attendance. They were absolutely correct in their thinking. I needed to think outside of a very big box. I simply had to commit to something more concrete, something that had legs, something that would close up the holes or missing links to an academic environment. If I played my cards right, I would be able to supplement and/or supplant every aspect of our organization that just wasn't serving our student population optimally.

CAS was depending on me to create the program I had dreamt about forever. If I succeeded, they would have a blueprint for additional afterschool programs on the secondary level. I didn't want to disappoint them, nor did I want to embarrass myself, my colleagues, or the wonderful community members who had recommended me for this extremely expensive experimental project. I was overwhelmed with the possibilities and the pitfalls. I was going to need more seats at the table. Maybe together, we could dig even deeper with these additional resources to send our program over the "top." I was aiming higher than ever before.

Chapter 27 – Uncharted Territory

I was shell-shocked, incredulous, and incredibly flattered at having been recommended to accept this CAS proposal by community activists on the Mt. Sinai Advisory Board. Although I had served on the board for a number of years, I couldn't believe that these well-placed individuals would consider putting this opportunity in the hands of my students, my staff, and, above all, myself. I began to dream about my wish list and felt like a kid in a candy store ready to load up my cart with goodies. Perhaps this program would finally be the answer to my prayers, making remediation and enrichment activities available to every student who needed and wanted to work harder. I knew the road to "all things possible" would be a long one, but that was my end game. Now we could all dig even deeper as a staff to really "aim high" for all kids.

Although I was in the middle of supervising summer school, I quickly notified my staff about this proposal, realizing that during the summer months, my teachers were scattered across many corners of the world. Yet, I knew that creating this program would be an "all hands on deck" situation, as we had no blueprint nor precedent to fall back upon, and there was no time to waste.

The meetings continued with the CAS liaison who would be based in my school to supervise the project. This young lady who appeared to be shy when I met her turned out to be an energetic and dynamic individual. She became my right hand in managing this huge endeavor. An incredible leader, her involvement complemented my work ethic in so many ways. We were both on the same page. Of course, she would need approval from the executives at the CAS Board as my requests from staff and students piled on my desk. Some of these requests were really "pushing the envelope" of what would be typical. However, I was given an extraordinary opportunity to change the face of what was acceptable, historical, and undeniably lacking in scope. We would be writing the playbook, and my impatience and excitement would require us to build the plane while we were flying it. If I were to put my whole being into bringing academic excellence to MCSM through this program, I needed it to fulfill the needs of the students and be absolutely certain that the staff would be on board.

Step one was to brief my faculty about this initiative, the mission of and vision for this entire package. I immediately sent out an assessment survey to everyone working in the building, asking for their input as to the types of enrichment they perceived as possible, value-added programs that would not only distinguish us from other traditional NYC high schools, but would provide the type of excellence that CAS had tasked us with envisioning. Suggestions ran the gamut from advanced classes to college prep, SAT and ACT tutoring sessions, art, music, and technology programs. They also included dreams of offering driver's education and study abroad programs, which would open new horizons for our students whose lives were limited to their neighborhoods and the ten-square-block area of our school community.

In September, we surveyed the kids as to their requests. I was amazed to see how insightful and cognizant they were of what was lacking in their academic day. For the most part, they were asking for classes that would help them graduate on time. The big question was...would they show up? Would they commit to a longer school day? For me to fulfill the requirements mandated by CAS, I needed to guarantee that students and staff would participate, not for the short term, but as an institutionalized part of a new extended school day. In other words, our new program would be expanded to 5:00 p.m., or even 6:00 or later.

This project in scope would be revolutionary for NYC high schools. We had always had afterschool academic tutoring programs and recreational and physical education activities, but never as an extension of the regular day. This "afterhours" school project would not serve as a means to supplant our regular classes. Rather, the entire morning and late afternoon programs would be linked as a seamless day in an attempt to customize our regular activities to better prepare our kids for college and the world of work. The "new" day would look and feel very different.

Remember, early on, we realized that the lack of instructional time was the primary factor in the high failure rate we had been experiencing. Traditionally, kids would become terribly frustrated when interrupted by the bell to change classes while in the middle of solving a problem and/or trying to comprehend a concept. Inasmuch as we couldn't stretch the normal school day any further than we already had, this extended day would give us that much needed extra time.

There were still many items to be worked out. Teacher pay and security for the program had not yet been addressed. In addition, while we were focusing on this CAS program, I had yet to deal with the unresolved issue of how to best help those teachers pulling down our scholarship year after year. I was pleased that this problem was getting smaller and smaller with each passing day, but it still seemed so wrong and unfair to the kids who deserved better. This was a deeply rooted roadblock to academic progress, common to so many schools nationwide, often thrown in the laps of the strong unions who were called upon to protect all of their members. I did appreciate all the assistance that the union leadership could provide to support our staff.

The beginning of a new school year would also welcome teachers with a series of repetitive, boring, and often useless professional development sessions. What a waste of time dealing with the bureaucratic nonsense. This year, for the first time, we spent the days instead planning for the extended school day with the Children's Aid Society. Groups of teachers brainstormed and created a voluntary task force that would come up with a plan. Perhaps I was the glue to make all their ideas gel together, as I briefed them at length about my own goals and objectives to be submitted into the required annual State Comprehensive Education Plan. Once again, however, the teachers were the ones who would truly create the framework. In general, my goal for staff was to empower everyone working in the school plant.

For this new school year we continued to eliminate the hated monthly faculty conferences where the principal would lecture for forty-five minutes. Just as in the previous year the teachers were asked to select professional development topics that they, themselves, found useful, and coordinate with their colleagues as to how to create a workshop. As an incentive to staff conducting these sessions, I allowed them to use this experience as an observation report, for which I wrote up an evaluation. Many jumped at this opportunity, and the new format of the meetings was better received than my lecturing on the first Monday of every month. For me, it was great not to have to watch over a hundred people fall asleep while I distributed administrative minutia. This change, I called progress. Of course, in today's world every teacher communicates with the administration via email and social media. The technology eliminates the need for meetings but does compromise the interaction of a close-knit staff.

Since this practice seemed to work well, we decided to do the same for the opening orientation days in September. These sessions offered the teachers the perfect opportunity to empower themselves, as well as others, in creating a new afterschool program soon to be renamed the "extended day," and eventually, God willing, the "regular day." How exciting this new endeavor was for the teachers since they were literally permitted to "run" the whole show! This was another "wow" moment for our school.

Before long, we had a preliminary plan for the afterschool program. My CAS liaison and I presented the framework to the executives funding this effort for their approval. Unfortunately, there were three major sticking points that had to be worked out in the existing plan. One of the most important issues was that of teacher pay. CAS offered to pay our staff only one-third of the hourly rate that I had anticipated. This was a major disappointment, one that could have put the entire program in jeopardy. What CAS funders failed to understand was that other funded afterschool programs sponsored by PSAL, Mt. Sinai, General Electric, IBM, and NYU College Bound paid our staff the same per-session salary as the Department of Education. I could not, in good faith, pay CAS staff a lower remuneration. Even if the teachers were willing to work for that lower amount, I couldn't agree. So many of my dedicated educators toiled voluntarily for years, tutoring kids after 3:00, during lunch, and before the start of the school day. Now it was time for them to have an extra income source. I wouldn't back down, but knew I had to proceed with caution. I wasn't about to look a gift horse in the mouth, but also knew that I had to be overly diplomatic in order to win them over.

After thoroughly explaining the issues of UFT union requirements and contracts, Department of Education bureaucracy, and the actual machinations of navigating a high school program, they reluctantly agreed to provide the hourly pay rate we were demanding.

The second sticking point was school security. CAS refused to pay for these added costs. They rightfully felt that the least the Department of Education could do was fund additional security officers for those necessary extended hours. Normally, the idea of risk and return would enter into the thought process, but not when you were dealing with the Department of Education. Considering the additional services CAS would be providing free of charge, compared to the cost of a few additional hours of pay for our security guards, the decision should have been a no-brainer. Beyond extending the school day, we were planning to open the school on Saturdays, Sundays, and holidays, taking time away from our own families to provide badly needed services for our kids, including opening up the computer room for those students who didn't have laptops. The technological divide was very personal for me.

The answer from the Department of Education was an unequivocal "No!" They told me to take these costs out of

176

my budget. Yet, you could be sure that if we would have an "incident," especially after school hours in or around the building, the board would have my *ass*, and make a case for lack of security. Then, suddenly the safety of kids would mean something to them.

CAS fought me on security costs for months. In the end, they did agree to provide some funding for security, but they weren't pleased. I know they did it for me, and I became more determined to make them proud by implementing a top-notch program.

The final sticking point was easier to address. I truly wanted to employ my staff and my staff alone for the program since these folks were familiar with the existing school culture and were in the best position to promote our school mission. I needed to feel comfortable with employing teachers I could vouch for in each classroom. Initially, the executives disagreed because they wanted to open up these positions to the entire city. We came to a compromise in that I would be able to fill these jobs with my staff first, but would be willing to open up positions to talented educators or expert resource personnel on the outside if we weren't able to fill them with our own. These professionals would be vetted as much as possible, be fingerprinted of course, and be given a lengthy orientation to the MCSM culture.

We all ended up winners. Our teachers filled the courses, and we were also able to attract professionals from Lincoln Center, neighboring colleges, museums, and theater companies. We were now good to go. We even had a group volunteer to teach Brazilian martial arts called "Capoeira" and celebrities from the American Ballet Theatre who became part of our enrichment programs.

Everyone seemed extremely excited about the prospect of a paid second job with badly needed additional income. We had numerous teachers and auxiliary personnel with special skills who dreamed about creating workshops, classes, and unique programs that, previously, had been out of the question due to budgetary constraints. Even now, with CAS looking at each of our requests for cost-effectiveness, we still had more flexibility than what we had been accustomed. In any event, attendance in each program remained the unanswered question. Would the kids attend?

Traditionally, our track record with running afterschool tutorials left a lot to be desired. We couldn't predict what would happen. Typically, the popular teachers and/or the ones who were effective in the classroom boasted higher numbers in these programs than their weaker colleagues. Case in point...our strongest history teacher ran a practice mock American History Regents exam on the last two Saturdays in May of that year. To our surprise, two hundred kids showed up. Whatever incentives or personal charm or chemistry that the teacher demonstrated in the classroom translated into a huge number of students buying into motivating strategies to get them to attend on a weekend. This teacher was consistent with his overall passing rate of over 90 percent on his exams and coursework thanks to his belief in kids, constant drilling, and "failure is not an option" approach to academic scholarship. I tried to clone this guy, but he was one of a kind when it came to demonstrating perseverance. He did manage to get the help from his fellow teachers by soliciting them to assist with the administration of these practice tests on the weekends. The movement caught on, and the excitement became contagious.

The negative folks in the school, of course, were least interested and swore that the kids would not stay after school anyway. However, with few exceptions, they were incredibly surprised at the numbers, as was I. Truthfully,

I tried at every turn to block, sabotage, or prevent in every way any teacher with poor classroom management, high failure rates, and poor attendance from teaching in this special program. I felt that a placement in this project had to be earned. Why would I waste precious funding on staff who couldn't bring in the numbers? In addition, why would kids sign up for classes in the afternoon with the same teachers that they had during the day that couldn't help them to raise their scholarship?

The program evaluators promised to scrutinize our attendance figures very carefully and, of course, cautioned us about yearly renewal if we didn't meet the guidelines or projections. The executives weren't convinced that by establishing a purely academic program that I was going to attain their minimum numbers. There would have been a greater guarantee had we agreed to throw out basketballs and open the school to the entire community, which was the typical objective of these kinds of programs in the past. MCSM had to create the model for other high schools, for which I would be extremely proud even in years to come.

Feeling the pressure to get kids to stay after school, we had to use every trick in the book to motivate them to enroll in any number of classes or activities that we offered. We had to remind ourselves that our students traveled from all over the city and needed a good hour or more to get home. During the late fall and winter months, it meant leaving the school in the dark and taking a very dangerous ten-block walk to the subway at Lexington Avenue and East 116th Street. Therefore, part of our outreach to students and parents had to include efforts to provide safety with a supervised community corridor to public transportation. Many of our teachers who were taking public transportation themselves were wonderful in escorting the kids to the train station. We needed peace of mind...always.

Regarding teacher placement in this prestigious program, naturally, it goes without saying, that several instructors got on my case and threatened to make an issue if denied a job. Minimally, they considered imposing grievances for any use of haphazard standards of seniority rules, which constituted a contractual regulation that I did have to respect. However, I realized that I might have an "out" because this was a new program and, technically, there was no prior seniority for our teachers or retention rights to consider. That is, unless they lumped together all afterschool programs as consideration for seniority. In the end I agreed to a compromise and extended the job offers to anyone who wanted to work with the understanding that attendance would be a major factor for retention, as would scholarship. I would not jeopardize this program to accommodate those people who couldn't take this project seriously.

Chapter 28 – The Gift
That Keeps on Giving

The gift of the Children's Aid Society put us on a path toward providing exceptional services to our students. I knew it was a beginning in our determination to create a level playing field for all of our kids. And, although my job wasn't simply to monitor the CAS afterschool program, since I had close to two thousand high school students, four hundred middle school kids, and a few hundred preschool and elementary school children under my watch, I decided to consider it an integral part of my regular workday, rather than a separate appendage of the educational program. On more days than not, I checked into my office very early, and from that time until 3:00 a million little things occurred—good, bad, and sometimes so ugly, it was difficult to imagine.

I determined that the same rigor, the same culture and work ethic, using the same standards, absolutely had to characterize the traditional school day as well as the extended day. I can't stress enough how lacking in rigor traditional night school and summer school classes were in terms of their overall passing requirements. I simply refused to allow this afterschool program to be an easy way out for the kids. I feared that kids would deliberately fail their day classes to be able to repeat the same classes after school in a less demanding, less rigorous setting. Both students and teachers had to agree to an MOU (Memorandum of Understanding) wherein it became clear that the classes offered in the CAS program were no less intensive, no easier than the classes they took during the regular school day. Hopefully, with this information in hand, deliberate failure would be avoided.

Much of the programming details regarding the scheduling of a very intricate and complex program from 3:00 to 6:00 daily was new to us. We were shooting for the stars, hoping to fill courses with students willing to stay well into the late hours. We created several overlapping and concurrent sessions. Scheduling two back-to-back classes of one and a half hours would have been very clean. In some cases, we were able to accomplish this feat. Students wanting to take two courses for credit would be able to manage that if they attended the program three days a week, receiving a full semester of credit upon completion. It became an administrative nightmare and real security risk when students wanted to attend the second session at 4:30 and not the first session at 3:00. Where would we safely house them until the second session? It dawned on us that we could use the computer labs, libraries, and gyms if we provided enough supervision. However, if this time wasn't scheduled, closely monitored, and taken seriously, it had the potential of being explosive. After all, these were high school kids with raging hormones, and there were many opportunities that could entice these adolescents to enter into bad behaviors. Alcohol, marijuana, and cellphone abuse were prevalent, fortunately on a small scale, but enough to cause scandals and much *agita* for me.

For Manhattan Center kids this new initiative bordered on the unknown and, initially, the students did not take it seriously. During the first few weeks, we did experience low numbers, which was to be expected. However, once the October report cards were released, the kids understood that the afterschool program was a safety net that would almost guarantee that they would graduate on time if they accumulated the necessary missing credits. We soon saw over five hundred kids attending each week. The variety of experiences offered morphed as the needs became apparent. Soon, we were opening the labs, computer rooms, gyms, and other facilities even on the weekends. As long as we had the working staff or volunteers to supervise the kids, the number of clubs, academic courses, and cultural experiences increased exponentially.

My own time became even more compromised, but at least I had something to show for it. My family's support allowed me to pop in to observe the goings-on within the program even on the weekends. The administrative staff hired to run the program was a real find and respected my vision of implementing a very rigorous college-bound initiative rather than a watered-down version of summer or night school programs. I knew I couldn't be present for everything, so certainly a reliable administrative team overseeing the credibility of the program was extremely critical. The reporting mechanisms put into place to make all the pieces of this puzzle transparent reassured me that the notion of "when the cat's away, the mice will play" would not be considered.

As the weeks and months passed, the administrative issues were resolved, and the preliminary reviews of the whole package were very favorable to us. Little by little, just about every kid in the school signed up for at least one class or initiative. More importantly, the executives of

CAS were pleased. After all, they had put big money on the line.

I joined a CAS networking group with other principals who had afterschool programs in their schools. Of course, I was the only one with a high school program, but I did pick up some strategies for the elementary school housed in my building. It is always beneficial to brainstorm with other professionals who are engaging in mutual sharing.

As I geared up for the next school year, I conducted a very detailed analysis, review, and self-evaluation of the entire project. Budgeting issues, personnel, academics, scholarship, and resources were all examined. For me, personally, I was concerned with the impact the extended school day was having on the traditional daytime program in raising all of my statistics. With my semi-annual review with the superintendent coming up, I needed some hardcore data and concrete evidence that this program was not a very costly and glorified babysitting service. In addition, before putting in my requests for the next school year, I needed to evaluate all of the standardized test results, SAT results, graduation results, and college admission data from our day school. I also wanted to issue a needs assessment survey for the coming year to the kids, parents, and staff.

Little by little, the jaw-dropping results became available. I expected improvement across the board, but an unexpected surprise was in store for me. At the time, I thought it might have been an anomaly or a blip in the system. The data showed that the weaker teachers with traditionally high failure rates who worked in the afterschool program showed remarkable improvements in scholarship. Their rate of failure plunged and their kids fared much better on the Regents exam. What changed? To be sure, it was too early to tell, but it was apparent that their involvement with the kids after school seemed to help their own self-esteem, making them more popular and believable, resulting in improved attendance. As the saying goes, "You have to be in it to win it."

It was truly rewarding for me to see teachers who had been struggling over the years emerge stronger and renewed simply by virtue of being a part of the CAS afterschool program. To be sure, some of these teachers would never be stars, but they were beginning to get the job done with respectable success. Improved attendance and the lowering of the cutting rate automatically translated into improved scholarship. At least I would have liked to think that this was the case. For the first time, I actually heard several say that they truly wanted to do better because it gave them a tremendous sense of satisfaction. It was also motivating for these folks to see their scores improve. Doing well was becoming very contagious. The fact is that our strength as human beings lies in our ability to compensate for the weak links in the chain and our ability to deal with all abilities, for better or worse. In an ideal world, we would be able to be all things to all people. We haven't yet achieved this perfect world in education. In the coming years, this observation was, indeed, substantiated. This was my *WOW* moment. I was ecstatic. "Never say never."

My physical education department, as I previously mentioned, was not happy with my decision to reduce the physical educational requirement from five to three periods per week for the students. And, although the agreement with CAS called for a fully academic program, I began to consider the idea that including some sports-related activities would enhance the quality of our afterschool offerings. Perhaps we could provide an additional carrot to keep kids in school and increase attendance. We already had PSAL funding for over twenty junior and senior varsity teams, but even these initiatives had numerous built-in budgetary restrictions.

I surveyed the physical education teachers as to which type of experiences they felt would draw better attendance. In the end, we were able to offer track and field experiences, bowling, Brazilian martial arts, hip hop, swimming, cheerleading, and more. The deal was that if they had sufficient participation, they would get the funding to continue in the future. This was a win-win situation because these activities provided a place for those students who only registered for the 4:30 afterschool session, keeping them out of trouble.

Finally, the science teachers were able to offer make-up labs for absentees in chemistry, earth science, biology, and physics. For students who needed more lab time to complete their write-ups, staying after school was the perfect solution.

The Regents exam scores in the sciences were off the charts when the results were reported in June. This improvement was a direct result of the number of kids who had completed the thirty-hour lab requirement and, in so doing, were able to sit for the test. Without providing make-up labs, we previously had no mechanisms built into our program for allowing absentees to make up the lab assignments. Nor were we able to provide the necessary time for those kids who couldn't complete their labs satisfactorily. Without completing the three-year science requirement, these kids couldn't graduate. It had been a Catch-22, but no longer was it a problem.

CAS made the impossible possible for MCSM. In fact, with so many youngsters completing a four-year science program, we were able to issue many more special diplomas at graduation called the Manhattan Center Endorsed Diploma. Since the city and state requirement was only a three-year sequence, completing four years in science was very, very prestigious. We continued to "aim high."

Chapter 29 – The Importance of Public/Private Partnerships

Long before the Children's Aid Society came into my life, Manhattan Center enjoyed a large number of collaboratives with private industry, community-based organizations, and neighboring universities. Considering that many of our kids began ninth grade verbalizing that there was little hope for them, having been raised in impoverished neighborhoods, with drugs and the sound of gunfire becoming normalized in their lives, we needed to address their feeling of helplessness. The many professionals who participated in our partnerships became the adult role models whom many of our students lacked in their lives.

Often, these mentors shared their own life experiences with the kids, which also included how they dealt with adversity. The students' involvement with our volunteers who came from similarly difficult circumstances gave them hope for the future by allowing them to see that through hard work and reaching out for the many opportunities afforded them, they too could look forward to success. Our participants made tremendous progress by virtue of their involvement in these collaboratives. For us, as middle-class adults, the realization that our school was truly a last-ditch effort toward a better life for our inner-city kids was humbling. We needed to immediately execute our vision of leveling the playing field for them. Everyone deserved the opportunity to dream. Little by little, the students did become more optimistic and hopeful thanks to these "miracle workers." Finally, there seemed to be a way out and "up."

I was extremely fortunate that the two principals who preceded me were totally onboard with creating collaboratives, reaching out to private industry leaders and universities. In fact, for a number of years, they had formed an advisory board of influential CEOs who, through their own networking abilities, were able to access opportunities and experiences that previously had seemed unimaginable for our inner-city students. Although these generous organizations looked to be as inclusive as possible, they were basically reaching out to the top echelon of students, those who were reliable and committed. I understood that they wanted to invest their time and resources in children who guaranteed them excellent outcomes. Nevertheless, I made it my mission to create other extracurricular activities, under the supervision of influential community role models, to which our needier kids might also apply and feel included.

Our Mt. Sinai Scholars Program was a real gem, with doctors and medical personnel taking time out of their busy schedules to mentor our students by providing experiences in preparation for a medical career. This Bridge to Medicine program created opportunities for over fifty students each year. Through endowments funded by very wealthy philanthropists, those participants who made the grade would receive full tuition for entry into the School of Medicine.

My tenure at MCSM allowed me to witness close to twenty years of earned opportunities for my kids because of the generosity of Mt. Sinai and their benefactors. The success of this program was largely due to the assistant principal assigned to coordinate these efforts, and several teachers working in the program.

Our General Electric Scholars Program and pre-scholars program served a few hundred kids each year. With one hundred mentors from General Electric, NBC, and its affiliate companies, these very busy role models provided academic, recreational, and college preparatory experiences for our students. These wonderful mentors took time out of their workdays to "adopt" our kids, make them a part of their families, and often create lifetime friendships. Hundreds of our kids managed to find job-shadowing activities, summer positions, internships, placement in the NBC Page Program, and even permanent assignments at GE and NBC in the New York area and throughout the country. It was a magnificent program with career opportunities in numerous industries of business, broadcasting, banking, technology, advertising, and the increasingly popular area of telecommunications. This collaborative, in comparison, incorporated additional students with a broad range of interests. However, with a large student population, there still was an insufficient number of opportunities to go around.

Fortunately, in addition to the GE Scholars Program, the parent company offered us an extremely generous three-year grant to fund our college-bound initiatives. Although the grant was to last only three years, my predecessor managed to extend the funding. When I took the helm, I convinced them to make the grant mine for life. In fact, the funding continued until the day I retired in 2004 because of the beautiful relationship established between the executives, our students, and our staff. The stage was set for a larger number of our students to dream.

My experiences visiting NBC Studios as a chaperone for the kids who were participating in the program were the highlight of my career. The level of respect that the NBC executives and mentors afforded me and my students was incredible. In fact, once I was literally dragged up to the twelfth floor of NBC at Rockefeller Center for a surprise. When I got off the elevator, I was greeted by the entire cast of *Friends* and invited to their celebration party. I nearly fell apart when I was introduced to these celebrities. I guess I'm a kid at heart.

We also had "sister" schools in Albuquerque, New Mexico, Lynn, Massachusetts, Louisville, Kentucky, and Raleigh, North Carolina. With visits to these communities, and the inclusion of visits to GE plants in Ohio and Erie, Pennsylvania, our college-bound network became an amazing way to share best practices.

The benefits of the GE Scholars Program brought with them incredible friendships for me as well. The president of NBC, and his wife, were frequent visitors to our school, and I was able to showcase the programs that GE had funded in person. They dropped by often enough to observe the goings-on, including the newly designed networked technology media labs. Each initiative provided all of the stakeholders with the opportunity to appreciate the fact that their monies and personnel were, indeed, making a difference. Our relationship was truly a blessing. Our kids really stood to benefit from this partnership.

In fact, as soon as the GE executives helped to get CNBC off the ground, we were invited to the facilities in New Jersey, to have lunch with all the famous anchors we see each day on their daily briefings. We were introduced to Brian Williams, Sue Herrera, and Ron Insana, who were impressed with our kids. We were all ready to jump ship and take on jobs with this new and exciting company. Without these folks, I could never have had the resources to give the kids these many value-added opportunities. The "scholars" program was created for this select group, but the other funding from GE went toward helping the entire school population.

The GE funding allowed us to create a photography darkroom and drama club studios for participation in the Manhattan Theatre Club program, in which our students were given the opportunity to not only see Broadway shows but to learn scriptwriting and acting from the professionals. This experience was so far out of their orbit that they were mesmerized by their contact with famous and talented people with this level of creative expertise.

With the GE funds we were also able to provide SAT preparation classes, college prep programs, state-of-the-art computer and technology classrooms, a rooftop greenhouse, enriching cultural activities, trips to college campuses, and virtually any activity that would enhance our academic potential and maintain the competitiveness of our students. The funding was carefully monitored so that it was used almost exclusively for student services rather than salaries. Our GE site coordinator was beyond extraordinary, and his leadership and collaboration paved the road to success for hundreds of kids. He even provided outreach to students in the middle school housed in our building by creating a junior scholars program. This project became a win-win for everyone since our older kids were able to mentor the younger ones and entice them into entering the GE program upon admission to high school. In addition, with the help of the GE network, we conferenced with other college-bound institutions in several other states, as a means to share best practices and engage in mutual visitation.

The importance of collaboration with community-based organizations, private industry, and communities of higher education cannot be overstated. To begin with, the much-needed funding and additional personnel that these programs provided helped to fill some of the gaping holes left by the unwillingness or frugality of the Department of Education. Occasionally, I could make the case for additional teaching units with which to create one or two more teaching positions or petition the district for textbook money.

By and large, I had more success by pounding the pavement and creating alliances with local politicians and community leaders. As mentioned earlier, I made friends with the members of the Police Benevolent Association to help the kids avoid involvement in gang activity, drugs, and criminal behavior. They even motivated our kids to pursue careers in law enforcement. I reached out to local universities in an effort to boost enrollment of our students into their programs.

The benefits of engaging with outside role models who had similar backgrounds to our students, and who were raised in similar neighborhoods as our kids, were incredibly powerful. We, as a school community, had the teaching and guidance skills to provide for our kids, but the career personnel working with our students were able to fill a void that we couldn't possibly understand. For this reason, it became my goal to encourage each and every student to sign on to work with an individual mentor or an organization after the regular school day.

Beginning in the ninth grade, we instituted a policy of logging on to a standardized resume given to each student in which to catalog his/her experiences. We kept it on file to be updated periodically for four years. This customized resource became a very useful tool when kids applied to college. The kids were never good at selling themselves or extrapolating their talents and skills to their advantage. Moreover, by the time they became seniors, they had forgotten what they had done as freshmen. This tool became a lifesaver, and their participation in these activities was another plus.

As a science and mathematics high school, we continually sought out additional potential collaboratives in the sciences and technology. We established partnerships with IBM and Cornell University Engineering Programs. They became beneficial initiatives for a select population. Funded through our GE grant, the Cornell University Synthesis Program opened the door to an engineering career for our students of color. Shamefully, in a prestigious school such as Cornell, less than one percent of entering freshmen for the engineering program were African Americans, Latinos, or females. With our students now having the ability to attend the Cornell Engineering Program during the summer and networking with the Engineering Department throughout the school year, we broke through that glass ceiling. I was proud to expand upon these programs, which were initiated by my predecessors.

Shortly after our initial entrance into Cornell engineering, the National Action Council for Minorities in Engineering (NACME) became active in our building, recruiting future engineers with the offer of Posse Scholarships (Portland Open Source Software Entrepreneurs). This foundation provided diverse groups of student leaders who worked in teams with a support network for the kids for four to five years. This team, or Posse, was another means of promoting this relatively unknown career path in engineering, especially for students who showed talent and potential, and more importantly, were often overlooked by traditional colleges.

In an attempt to be all things to all students, I realized that I owed it to my profession and to the youngsters to also promote teaching as a career. Early on in my story, I mentioned PROJECT MUST, which I inaugurated before I became principal. This program is certainly worthy of mentioning a second time since all the goings-on at MCSM are reflections of great teaching. The kids were astute enough to realize that teachers were not high up on the income ladder. Nevertheless, when polled, there was enough interest in pursuing this career route. Together, we made contact with NYU and found out that they had a doctoral program with candidates who were willing to head up a collaborative program.

One of the more influential professors at the university was able to secure funding to create a mentoring program. The initiative, called "MUST," stood for Mentoring Urban Students for Teaching. In designing the program, I wanted to tap into the middle school housed in our building. I realized that if we were going to encourage our kids to be teachers, it would make sense to have younger kids for them to teach. I created a model whereby four junior high school classes would work with our high school program interns. Mentoring and tutoring services were provided. For two days per week, the kids from both programs would work together, and on the third day I would team up with two doctoral candidates from NYU as we offered our kids teaching strategies in a Teaching 101 introductory class. Wow! This was powerful! The high school kids had the advantage of working closely and personally with me and with two NYU teachers. In addition, as a fringe benefit, they had all the amenities of the college campus and facilities.

By the way, this initiative was one of many collaboratives that would offer our kids college credits while attending high school. This newly acquired gift was separate and apart from the college credits our kids were earning in Advanced Placement classes.

When I became principal of MCSM in 1995, I refused to give up teaching in PROJECT MUST. While it continued to be exciting for the kids to have their principal as their teacher, for me it was an excellent way to keep close contact with the youngsters. Moreover, the curriculum we unlocked for the students regarding how to teach in an inner-city school gave the kids a "behind the scenes" look at what really goes on in a very bureaucratic environment. The kids were often in shock upon hearing stories of events that went on in school on a day-to-day basis. The program also helped to build bridges with the junior high school, allowing us to vet potential incoming MCSM students.

Many other administrators would shudder at the thought of having an elementary and middle school housed in their high school building, but I was committed to take full advantage of this very unique setup. To this day, this joint effort was one of my favorite projects, not only because I was directly involved in teaching within the program, but because I was able to tap into a different segment of the school population. Later on I was able to offer teaching positions at MCSM to the graduates of this initiative. Imagine if every high school in the city would create a similar program; we would have an incredibly large pool of applicants for future teaching positions. These many years later, attracting qualified candidates to teach in the New York City public schools remains a challenge.

In a continued effort to bring every student into some sort of partnership, I again sent out student surveys, assessing their needs or wishes for additional clubs or programs. Ideas came out of the woodwork. Our CAS funding allowed us to be somewhat frivolous with our spending.

One of the first requests was from a transgender student who was suggesting a Gay/Straight Alliance club. When he approached me with this idea, he was expecting a negative response. Even in the 1990s, I was very progressive and believed that children should be proud of their identities. To his surprise, I said "absolutely." The agreement was that there had to be an adult coordinator present for every session. Wisely, I stepped up security for the club, just in case there might be student, or even faculty, backlash. No one protested and the club boasted sixty members. In fact, when they asked whether they might attend the prom as cross-dressers, again, I responded in the affirmative. It was their prom, and the only thing that really mattered was that every attendee behaved appropriately.

After the formation of this club, the kids decided to push the envelope yet further. Requests came my way for the formation of a Christian Club. In addition, our Muslim population was requesting a club and space where they could pray. Although I welcomed these ideas, I had to do my homework with regard to the legality of creating such clubs before I gave my final answer. With the idea of separation of Church and State on the books, I needed to receive approval not only from my superintendent but also from the State Education Department of New York. I documented all of my calls with State Education personnel. The final decision ruled in my favor and both clubs would be permitted as long as staff members would be present in each classroom. In addition, the agreement would include a guarantee that the teachers overseeing the clubs would not engage in proselytizing or in conducting religious activities. The teacher was merely in the room to guarantee the club members' safety.

With the backing of the State, my superintendent gave me the go-ahead.

The students were beyond appreciative, but the staff, not so much. The majority of the teachers were fine with the formation of these clubs because they were extremely child-centered and liberal. There were a few hysterical staff members who immediately complained to the union. Fortunately, the complaint went nowhere and the clubs proceeded as planned, although I strictly cautioned the coordinators that they were not to promote the clubs in any fashion and that these activities needed to be purely student-run. Another milestone was accomplished!

These kids had an affiliation, a self-esteem booster, and another carrot to keep them in school. Soon, we added an Asian Club, a Latino Club, and an African Studies Club. Before long, everyone was participating in some initiative. I suspect that many of these clubs today would invite controversy given the climate of racial injustice in this country. From my point of view the current climate is the very reason why we need to have such programs in every school. I have always been extremely proud of every initiative created for MCSM students to prepare them to participate in a global society. Considering that we prioritized math and science courses we were also offering five second language opportunities for the kids to pursue. Our foreign language department provided a three- to five-year sequence in Spanish, French, Latin, Japanese, and Sign Language.

Within the year, we had formed twenty new clubs and had twenty-two varsity teams and numerous academic college preparatory afterschool programs. This school was "rockin" big time!

There was one additional unique partnership that I must mention. The "Bridge the Gap" program was a fundraising effort led by a number of female philanthropists from NYC who had heard about our school from serving on various advisory boards, including Mt. Sinai. This unique group of volunteers recognized that although many of our students received prestigious scholarships and financial aid packages from Harvard, Tufts, Brown, or Cornell, they often lacked those initial funds necessary to commute, set up their dorm rooms, or enjoy the basic joys of college life. For these students who had worked so hard to defy the odds and overcome adversity to be forced to decline acceptance to their desired university because the remaining financial burden was too great was a travesty. By hosting teas, auctions, and cocktail parties, the "Madison Avenue Ladies," whom I nicknamed, became benevolent friends of MCSM and gave these kids the special funding earmarked specifically for the costly incidentals needed to begin their college careers. Once again, the public/private partnership proved to be an asset to our school community.

At this point so many of our youngsters were already benefitting from the services offered on the local college campuses including Hunter, City (uptown, downtown), NYU, Polytechnic, and Columbia. With access to their libraries and media rooms the kids already felt like college material. In many cases our students were allowed to audit classes for free, and in other cases they were even offered college credit.

These incredible partnerships put smiles on many faces including those of students, parents, staff, and the mentors who enjoyed giving back. The lifelong friendships made, and the numerous ways in which our students were finally able to see a future, cannot be minimized.

These activities need to be the essence of every school to help their kids succeed.

Considering the fact that children spend more time in school than at home and that educators are tasked with preparing our students to become the next generation of productive citizens, it is unacceptable that the public schools continue to be the stepchild of our society's resources. As a principal, it became increasingly obvious to me that the operating costs provided by the Department of Education were barely sufficient to offer basic services to our students.

The bloody truth here is that principals were never prepared to take on this responsibility. The need to secure the support of our community leaders in helping to create a beneficial educational organization was never discussed in any course we were ever required to take.

As a final note here, it would be extremely helpful to include several courses leading to certification as an educational administrator to be devoted to the art of building partnerships with the community. We were never prepared to lead in this area. We as educators do not have the tools or the knowledge to prepare kids for the world of work, as we have been removed from this environment for many years. Students in high school need the benefit of mentors working in the field who can provide job shadowing and career planning. Once again, the courses needed for certification as a teacher and/or administrator missed the mark in preparing instructional leaders to meet the challenges of educating in inner-city schools. I'm so glad my colleagues and I were willing to dig deep and aim high for the sake of our students.

Chapter 30 – The Living Room

With the success of the public/private partnerships and the CAS afterschool program, thinking outside of the box was becoming contagious. With an enhanced budget, hardworking staff members, engaged students, and parents who supported our vision, we had the right ingredients to truly move our organization forward. I could never anticipate who would approach me next for a piece of the pie. When the project was first introduced to me, and we formed a task force to gather ideas, there was some guarded pessimism as to the possibility of buy-in from staff and kids, knowing that they would be committing several hours per week beyond the traditional day.

Now, I had to turn people away because we just couldn't afford to do everything. We actually compiled a wait list of programs that we could "swap" in should we have to dissolve any of the existing classes because they were no longer cost-effective or lacked sufficient attendance. Even more surprising was that student interest was so high that I often found kids milling around after the afternoon session ended, refusing to go home even after 6:00. We did have staff who volunteered to continue teaching into the evening hours because they were so determined to help the kids. I literally had to kick them out of the building.

At this point, I had to make a more genuine effort to control our CAS budget, since spending was reaching our limit. Yet the next request was an initiative I just couldn't refuse. One of my mathematics instructors asked to meet with me to thoroughly walk me through his proposal. It would take quite a bit of time to discuss its nuances. This guy did his research, had already conferenced with his department colleagues, and had prepared answers to the many questions he had anticipated from me. He envisioned the creation of a "living room" in a large, unused area in the basement, which had been a woodworking shop many years ago. The reasoning behind this request came from his morning meetings with fellow mathematics colleagues. During their discussions, they came to the conclusion that even with the added time we had built in for math classes, there was a persistent inability for a large number of students to master the more difficult topics encountered in subjects such as algebra, geometry, and trigonometry. These same deficiencies were commonly observed by each teacher and continued to be problematic for the youngsters. This instructor had previously worked in private industry as a buyer for a large department store. He felt that he could transfer some of his successes in the business world into teachable moments with this plan.

His vision for the "living room" was a comfortable place where students needing help in a particular area of problem solving would find master teachers, student tutors, and coordinators ready to customize a plan for each individual's improvement. The student would need a referral from the math teacher with an actual appointment. The room would be filled with donated couches, chairs, and tables to create an unintimidating and inviting decor. It seemed like a fantasy. However, this school was created to encourage dreamers, and so I agreed to allow the program to go forward, not really knowing how well it would be received by the students, nor how costly it would be to our pocket. To my amazement, within the first few weeks, there wasn't a chair to be had! The room was flooded.

Coincidentally, shortly after the initiation of this "room," which the kids wanted to be modeled after our Manhattan coffee lounges, I received an unannounced visit from the chancellor of the Department of Education. It was very frightening to me that without prior preparation the person in the highest office at the DOE would be observing me in action. I wasn't really concerned that he would be dissatisfied with our programs or building maintenance, but these surprise visits made my adrenaline kick in, as I never knew what we'd come upon during our walkaround. At least with announced visits I could spend weeks mobilizing the troops to prepare and alert the kids to stay out of the halls.

With this unanticipated arrival of our guest, hopefully, we wouldn't stumble upon two kids having sex in the stairwell or hear a teacher curse out a student because he didn't turn in his homework assignment. Yes, those situations did occur. I was also concerned that I would receive a major reprimand for having converted the schoolyard into a parking lot for the staff who were tired of getting parking tickets on the street. I had known that this illegal use of the yard might someday come back to haunt me especially since I had never let the DOE know about it, but my teachers were constantly arriving late to their first period class because of the lack of legal parking spots in the vicinity of the school. I had to address the issue with a solution. However, to my surprise, instead of citing me for breaking the law, the chancellor actually thanked me for making room in the yard for his driver to park his car alongside the other staff vehicles. I dodged another bullet!

As we circulated around the school observing classes, programs, and kids engaged in many diverse activities, I decided to introduce him to the "living room." He couldn't quite grasp the concept until we actually entered the room and, to his shock and pleasure, saw youngsters tutoring youngsters who were totally engaged in the academics. Everyone seemed to love this notion of "each one, teach one." He thought it was a brilliant idea. So brilliant, in fact, that he asked our coordinator to do a demonstration lesson at the chancellor's monthly staff meeting, which included all the superintendents in the city. I was flattered and extremely nervous at the same time.

Aside from receiving a glowing evaluation from the chancellor, he was able to help me out of a potentially difficult situation.

Prior to the chancellor's visit, plans were being finalized for the members of our GE Scholars Program to visit NBC Studios for dinner and a kickoff event. That morning, it was announced that an NBC news anchor had received an envelope of anthrax delivered to his office. How could I possibly allow these kids to enter a building that could have a potential anthrax contamination? The Department of Education would have had my head on a silver platter if I had allowed the visit without the chancellor's approval. I seriously doubted that this permission would be forthcoming. The timing, however, was perfect since his unexpected visit to my school allowed me to explain the situation, to which he gave me an immediate go-ahead. To say I was flabbergasted was an understatement. Having worked for over thirty years in an educational bureaucracy that exuded a "gotcha" attitude, this chancellor was a breath of fresh air.

The "living room" continued to be a huge success. The teacher coordinator who first introduced this concept would eventually go on to become a principal at a Bronx school. He was, after all, a standout guy, a consummate educator and businessman. He knew how to negotiate with kids, and his experiences proved instrumental in appealing to the student mentors to buy into his motivating incentives to tutor. At the same time, his gentle approach with students in need of remediation encouraged them to attend these valuable learning sessions. By the way, our demonstration lesson at the chancellor's office with the superintendents did go very well. I added another feather in my cap, and certainly one for our coordinator. Every element of the "Living Room" program was wonderfully received, but not without much *agita* prior to the visit.

The results on the Regents math exams in June were very impressive. Once again, a passionate staff using creative ways of boosting academic performance, along with a willing population of kids in need of assistance, produced the synergy necessary to make a difference. With time and money well spent, we were finally beginning to accomplish our mission for Manhattan Center—not just for some, but for almost everyone. We were beginning to reap the rewards of digging deep and aiming high.

Chapter 31 – Big Brother Is Watching You

Each day, as with most schools, the number of transactions, activities, decisions, and goings-on were too great to count. The marathon schedule requiring me to hop from one bell to another, putting out fires, satisfying community requests, and just trying to survive this "educational circus" left little time to actually smell the roses. As we began to enjoy some very significant academic results and major changes in our culture, especially with the new way of delivering instruction, we failed to notice that we were being observed by many within and outside of the educational community.

Our collaboratives, the first high school-based Children's Aid Society program in the city, our block scheduling, and increased instructional time were sending shockwaves throughout the city, creating a sense that something very significant was going on in our building. People were noticing. Although our reputation for outstanding academic performance had begun with our first graduating class in 1986, and continued for many years thereafter, it wasn't until now that we lived up to our promise of delivering true academic success for everyone. Yes, the previous classes did graduate, the kids did receive a diploma, and most received acceptances into college. However, now we felt as if we were reaching a much larger audience and were setting the bar even higher, thanks to a hard-working and persevering faculty willing to dig very deep. We didn't just raise expectations. We were able to deliver.

As the saying goes, "things happen when you least expect them." One day each year many schools participated in a citywide event with someone important and significant in the outside world who literally took charge of the organization. In an attempt to build partnerships, this influential person shadowed the "real" principal during this special time. While observing a leadership class on advocacy with our "Principal for a Day," who was Suzanne Wright from NBC, there was a knock on the door. When the teacher opened the door, a six-foot-seven gentleman asked to speak to me immediately. The teacher informed him that I was with a very special guest and was quite busy interacting with kids in a lesson. Not taking "no" for an answer, the teacher allowed him to enter the room to explain to me that he was representing Caroline Kennedy Schlossberg, who wished to speak to me.

The daughter of a former United States president was waiting outside of the room anxious to talk to me? I was immediately embarrassed at my initial hesitation to allow this gentleman in, but extremely honored to have such a prestigious visitor in our midst. My NBC partner and I walked out to greet this lovely person, and we had a beautiful conversation about our Principal for a Day program and Manhattan Center. Ms. Kennedy was extremely enthusiastic about everything she heard.

I couldn't help but explain to our unexpected visitor that we had met before while touring the Greek island of Crete. It was many years earlier, and we bumped into each other while exploring the Caves of Knossos. I'm not sure she believed me, but, with a great sense of humor, said, "It's nice seeing you again."

A week later, I received a book of her mother's favorite poems as a gift. She even wrote a personal inscription to me. It was an overwhelming experience.

Within time, I began receiving invitations to sit on a number of advisory boards. Although my time was already stretched thin, I took it as an honor and hoped the networking would work to my advantage. Securing more projects and "stuff" for my kids was enough motivation for me to be willing to be shot out of a cannon. Before long, I had a seat on the Mt. Sinai Advisory Board, the Hunter College Board, the Polytechnic Institute Board, the NYU Board, and the Children's Aid Society Advisory Board. Fortunately, these groups only met one evening per month, but still often conflicted with my regular evening functions at school. We had our own advisory councils at school and, with PTA meetings, award ceremonies, sporting events, and other activities, the job truly required from me more hours than I had in a day. In addition, how could I miss the debate team's competitions on Saturdays? Actually, one of our celebrated NBC anchors, Jane Pauley, put together the Forensic Debate Team for my school, and I couldn't let her down.

My life was very full, and, fortunately, my health was good as I had recently turned fifty. I was still able to chase the kids down the hall and climb the steps two at a time.

My superintendent, and even the chancellor, knew that if they requested anything from me my answer would always be, "I got this."

The surprises didn't end there. One morning, I received a call from a famous singer who was also the daughter of one of the greatest male vocalists to ever live. Nancy Sinatra was requesting to use my auditorium and dressing rooms for an upcoming block party fundraiser hosted by a world-renowned Italian restaurant, which was across the street from my school. I used to think these were prank calls, but after getting a visit from a member of a president's family I had to think twice.

Of course, I couldn't say "no." I filled out the proper papers for the usage of school facilities, which I sent downtown, and complied with the requests she made. As a form of thanks, she gave me two invitations to the event. Of course, we attended, and my wife and I were surrounded by celebrities from the entertainment world.

Following these experiences, I received a call from NBC asking for permission to film some episodes of *Law & Order: Criminal Intent* in my school.

With NBC being a partner of ours, it was a no-brainer. So, the crew took over my office, which required me to temporarily move out. Several classrooms and the hallways were also used, making those areas off-limits to the kids. It was a truly exciting experience and, best of all, we received a $4,000 honorarium for each filming session, with which we were able to bolster our programs.

During this period of filming, a very funny incident occurred. I must confess that as a frustrated actor, I really wanted to have a role in one of the episodes, but I knew that wouldn't be possible. However, had this been a comedy series, I probably would have gotten a role as the crazy principal because, at one point, I thought I was losing my mind.

Coincidentally, and unbeknownst to me, as they were filming an episode about a fire taking place in a school, an actual fire was blazing across the street. All of a sudden, uniformed firemen entered the building with me thinking they were part of the acting cast. I proceeded to tell them that the dressing rooms were to the right, and in that location they could join the rest of the group to change their clothes. The firemen thought I was totally out of my mind and couldn't understand why I was asking them to join any group to change their uniforms. When they finally explained that there was a real fire going on across the street, and they needed to use my building to shelter those displaced by it, I had a lot of explaining to do to the NYC Fire Department. When I told them that I was the principal, they thought I had a few loose screws. We all had a good laugh.

At times, I thought we were turning my building into a Hollywood set. On another occasion, I thought I was dreaming when I bumped into actress Meryl Streep in my lobby following a filming crew. What was this occurrence all about? Apparently, without my knowledge, they were filming a scene from *Music of the Heart*, a true story about the violin program in our River East elementary school. A very prestigious program was created to promote music education in the district. With the monetary support of famous artists and musicians in the industry, the kids were taught to play the violin and ended up performing at Carnegie Hall. What a thrill!

In fact, as a side benefit, another world-famous actress and entertainer who was originally selected to play a role in the movie had been secretly entering my building early in the morning to receive violin instruction. I never imagined having to provide security for her or any other celebrity. It was incredible to be up close to this very popular singer, but I had to pretend that she was just like any other staff member. Until this day no one in my faculty knew this was happening. I was sworn to secrecy. I will not divulge her name.

I had to be grateful that every so often someone exciting and out of the ordinary knocked on our doors to break up our very routinized day. A very young substitute teacher who was working in our River East Elementary School housed in our building came into my office one sunny day. She was very small and thin in stature and would probably have passed for a high school senior. In any case, she stopped by to ask me if I would put her on the top of the "sub list" because she wanted to work as many days as possible. I really would have preferred to hire her full-time as a teacher, but because she was an aspiring actress, she could not commit. Of course, I agreed to help her, especially because her relationship with kids was superlative. Who would have known that this little lady asking for more hours of work would end up being Kerry Washington, the star of a television series, a film actress, a producer and director, and an activist and author? This incredibly accomplished person actually sat in my office talking to little old me. I am worse than the kids when it comes to being near famous people. So here we have another noteworthy anecdote in the life of a principal.

Over the years I stumbled upon so many unexpected situations with the many circles of former students, faculty, and corporate partners with whom I networked. In the spring of 1998 I received an invitation to a reception being given in my honor at the Metropolitan Museum of Art. The Settlement College Readiness Program, a community-based organization serving our schools, was recognizing me for my service to East Harlem. I graciously accepted their award and brought my family to the ceremony. As I entered the facility a young lady approached me to offer her congratulations. At first glance I hadn't recognized her, but upon noticing the necklace she was wearing, which was a Christmas present from me many years ago, I realized that this person was my darling Connie from my middle school in the Bronx. We had not seen each other in a while, and now a mother of three all grown up, her smile returned. As a loyal subscriber to the programs at the museum, Connie had read about my honoring and wanted to surprise me. This evening would never be forgotten.

With so much going on in school, my time with my family was continuously compromised. The school building was now open seven days a week for sports team practice, for library services, and for technology-related activities. Many students were able to utilize the science labs. In the spring, the classrooms were filled on weekends with SAT and ACT coaching sessions, Regents review classes, and other remedial or mock testing sessions for improvement. True, I wasn't mandated to be there in person, as the kids were always supervised by a teacher, but my ultra-responsible nature pushed me to travel in most weekends to see that activities were calm and orderly. Besides, I simply loved being surrounded by kids doing great things.

Another reason for my frequent off-hour visits was the fact that safety conditions in many of our facilities were below standard. I was always worried about the welfare of our students. Most people outside of education, or at least those alien to the inner-city school climate, fail to realize that the physical working conditions in many of the schools are abysmal and downright dangerous. A number of buildings were built in the early 1900s, were not always updated, had no air conditioning, had crumbling internal and external construct, and were riddled with vermin and roaches.

Manhattan Center was built in 1941 and was much in need of repair. Each morning as I entered my office, I interrupted a group of mice munching on my papers. With each step, I heard the scattering of water bugs. It was a sickening way to begin a workday, having to sweep mice droppings from my desk. Repeated sprayings, positioning of mouse traps, and setting out sticky paper to paralyze the mice had limited success. The laws relating to poison control in schools prevented me from using stronger substances, and so it persisted.

To say that this was an unhealthy work environment is an understatement, but it was exacerbated by the arrival of spring. When the weather warmed up, I was able to open the windows in my office to get some fresh air. One day, I arrived to find squirrels sitting on my desk. This coincided with the beginnings of my breathing problems. Soon I was experiencing shortness of breath and severe congestion. I had to take the elevator instead of the stairs and could no longer chase the kids through the hallways. I was worried. I sought out the care of a cardiologist as well as a pulmonologist. Neither specialist could figure out what was going on and nothing showed up on the scans. I decided to seek the advice of an allergist who inquired as to my home and work environment. When I explained the condition of my office, with the mice and squirrels, he knew that the workplace was the answer. In addition, the squirrels were building nests on the outside windowsill, and I was also inhaling the garbage they carried.

I immediately called the Environmental Protection Agency, OSHA, and the Department of Education officials, with little response or concern on their part.

It was only when I threatened to go to the *New York Times* and to speak with my friends at NBC to inform them of these horrendous conditions did I finally get results. Considering that the kids spent much time in my office for meetings, they too were in danger. It took a good six months for me to return to my usual self. No one should have to accept these working conditions. In any case, I needed to see that my students were okay, especially after hours and on weekends when many of the maintenance folks did their cleaning and repairs. In the dead of winter, the rooms were not adequately heated, and icicles formed on the windows. In my twenty-one years at the plant, the radiators were bled many times but still failed to provide consistent warmth. Some classrooms were freezing, while others were blazing hot. It was common practice to move groups of students from room to room or from facility to facility to provide them with the warmth, proper ventilation, and necessary comfort conducive to learning. How could I not check in on them as often as possible? They were "my kids."

Chapter 32 – The Value-Added
Benefit of Parent Advocates

So much has been said over time about the value of parental involvement, or lack thereof, in a high school environment. For many suburban school districts, parental involvement often results in their constant helicoptering over their children, teachers, and administrators. This sense of entitlement allows them to make personal, often unrealistic, requests, as though the public schools were their private domain.

I imagine that accepting this practice is the price you pay to work in a well-to-do school district, with a salary scale surpassing that of NYC teachers and administrators by 25 percent or more. Setting aside this elite mentality, parental participation in the suburban schools helped these schools to offer their students unimaginable resources and amenities. Everyone had a computer, everyone had the most up-to-date set of textbooks, and equipment covered the latest innovations in technology. The campus facilities included lavish stadium-style seating with soccer, football, and baseball fields galore. On the streets of New York City we had to share the meager park facilities with the entire community, and frequently had to call upon police to remove the drunks, addicts, and gang members so that our teams could play.

For us in the city schools, expectations of parental involvement varied from place to place, and in many cases a very low bar was set. For starters, being in East Harlem, our school was located at least one mile from a subway station. Car ownership was a rarity. Furthermore, with a very large segment of the school population coming from outside of the neighborhood, the prospect of parental participation was rather bleak. To add to the problem, a large number of parents were non-English speakers. My fluency in Spanish would certainly be an asset, and believe me, it did make a huge difference. It still was not enough to engage these very needy parents. In addition, since close to 100 percent of our kids qualified for Title One programs, the income level of the parents would not help fill our coffers. To add to these challenges, many of our students came from single-parent homes, or were being raised by grandparents or by no natural parents at all. In fact, a small number of our students were completely homeless. Sadly, it is estimated that there are currently over 100,000 homeless school children in New York City.

We had to work with what we had. Again, I relied on my staff to help me come up with revolutionary ways to increase parental involvement, in spite of the transportation challenges, childcare responsibilities, work schedules, and income levels.

My administrative assistant, Sandra, was a "wiz" at building a parent base and was responsible for much of what we accomplished with parents. As mentioned previously, Sandra always had my back. She communicated with me constantly, even at home, to give me a heads-up when there were rumblings in the community. An expert in technology with a lifetime of commitment to community service in the metropolitan area, she was a dynamo in being able to merge the two, providing a tremendous amount of networking ability. Sandra seemed to know everyone. As an extremely generous and compassionate person, whom we nicknamed "Saint Sandra," the kids and parents flocked around her desk on a daily basis.

One day, Sandra approached me with an idea. Coming from the most trusted individual I had ever met, my eyes were wide open to her suggestion. Apparently, over time, Sandra had received numerous requests to provide computer skills training in word processing, and to create email accounts for parents in the community. Sadly, of course, these parents didn't actually own a computer, so their requests included a need to use our devices and facilities. Sandra wanted to create a technology class for the parents, which she would be willing to teach.

I found the idea brilliant! It was a win-win! I handed her the ball knowing that she would run with it for miles and score a touchdown. Before long, an impressive number of parents had signed up and, at the end of the semester, each parent received a Certificate of Excellence for their completion of Sandra's class. Although Sandra thanked me for putting so much faith in her efforts, it was I who needed to extend my thanks to her. In essence, the theory of "each one, teach one" became contagious within our school culture now even for parents, and this class became institutionalized into the Manhattan Center mission, educating parents to improve the lives of their entire family.

The next extraordinary idea came from my senior class student advisor. Knowing that parents had so little time to spare especially after the workday, she suggested providing a light dinner for them, so that coming to evening events would be easier. Also, with the acknowledgment that an added challenge to attending PTA meetings stemmed from lack of childcare, she recruited students to entertain the youngsters, providing babysitting services while we conducted the workshops. The final jewel in this plan related to transportation for the parents and children. She was able to secure bus passes to cover transportation and, later, provided school buses to transport these families for special school events. With all of these components put into place, we increased the number of parent participants at the meetings exponentially. Their commitment to attending the PTA sessions allowed me to further their involvement by inviting them to sit on my leadership and advisory boards, thus cementing the parent advocate relationship with MCSM.

These parent leaders became essential to the well-being of our school community. Their influence extended well beyond the school plant, and their allegiance to me proved to be invaluable.

Sadly, however, hiring practices, interviewing, and recruiting for teaching positions did not involve our parents. Outside of the city, parents are often recruited to sit on interviewing panels to screen candidates for vacant slots. Our hiring system was primarily based on seniority. Often we were forced to "bump out" exemplary teachers in exchange for U-rated instructors with more seniority who were sent from the borough high school office. I had "zero" say in the decision. It killed me each time to have to accept teachers whose prior history was unknown to me, but my protests did nothing to change the situation.

The combination of Civil Service regulations maintained by the city and union contractual requirements created an environment in which teachers were often circulated from school to school, borough to borough, without regard for the effect they were having on the students. In one case, I was forced to accept a teacher who had been dismissed from ten schools! This was unconscionable! Some of the files of these teachers read like the "Great American Novel," full of tragic situations involving children, both physically and emotionally. I know that in many districts outside of the city, parents would absolutely not accept these archaic regulations governing this delivery of instruction by our professionals. Some of our devoted parents would have served well on these interviewing panels.

I had no choice but to accept these unsatisfactory teachers, but I did have a choice when it came to documenting their inadequacies in my school. To be fair, I gave myself at least a year to assess their ability to teach and work with kids. With very few exceptions, they were not showing improvement. In most cases there was a similar pattern from job to job, and I finally had to break the cycle of passing them along to someone else. Instead of trying to remove them, only to be transferred to another school to destroy more lives, I decided to do what was necessary to change the climate.

In certain very unfortunate circumstances where criminal activity was involved, the Office of Special Investigations Unit would remove the individual or place him/her in the "rubber room" far from the children. This "rubber room" was an office where teachers who were being charged with improprieties were placed while receiving their full pay. Their stay in the "rubber room" in some cases lasted over five years until the legal pathways were fully exhausted and a decision was made as to their future. Can you imagine being paid for five years to sit in an office doing nothing? Amazing how many employees exist who are rewarded for failing the system. Fortunately, years later the "rubber room" was gone, and personnel removed from classrooms or a traditional school setting are currently assigned to offices to do paperwork until their case is resolved.

All told, I found myself in this uncomfortable situation a couple of times during my tenure as principal. I will admit, however, that there were cases throughout the city where employees were put in this room unfairly. I guess it works both ways. Not every administrator is credible or discreet. Perhaps the real failure came from the lengthy amount of time it took to resolve these issues one way or the other. In any case, we need to do a much better job in vetting educators who work with kids before placing them in schools. Nationwide there are just too many scandals.

One of these situations, in particular, was noteworthy, as it did ultimately involve the parents.

A teacher with many years of experience had been transferred to my school, having been removed from several other schools because of incidents of poor discipline and a high student failure rate. The teacher had been accused of "unacceptable" behavior against several students in another school. This incident was not enough to require dismissal, so they brokered a "deal," which was a transfer to my school because I was told that I could handle this individual.

During the first semester 95 percent of the ninth-grade students failed the course with only several kids passing the class. Nothing could justify such outcomes. However, the instructor convinced me that teaching brighter students in a physics honors class the next semester would be better. Determined to give this person every chance to prove me wrong, I agreed. I took a chance since the top students in the school were often more tolerant, were better behaved, and had a longer attention span. This time, the teacher failed 100 percent of the students for the first quarter. Mind you, these kids had incredible

GPA scores. Over 90 percent of these kids were applying to prestigious colleges with scholarships. They knew that their acceptance into these schools depended on the outcomes of this honors class. I predicted correctly that they would be hurt by the inability of this teacher to be successful with the youngsters.

My calls to the district office went nowhere. My pleas for removal were met with their advice to "document everything." All well and good, but that didn't resolve the issue of what these kids were going through in this class. Removal of an instructor required two years of unsatisfactory ratings. These kids didn't have two years to wait. They deserved better.

The importance of parent advocates became even more apparent with the situation at hand. When the parents of students in this class became aware that my superiors were not acting quickly enough regarding the teacher's removal, they insisted on meeting instead with the instructor. As expected, the meeting did not go well. The parents tried to reason with this employee, offering help and suggestions for better success. The teacher was inflexible, and just did not "get it." Out of desperation, the parents followed with a letter-writing campaign and petition to have the instructor removed, at any cost.

Fortunately, several of the more active parents in the school had friends at the *New York Times* and knew that this situation could go public at any time. Keeping that possibility in mind, they decided to hand-deliver a huge pile of letters and signed petitions from the parents of all of the students involved to the personnel office with the threat of publicizing this travesty if nothing were done.

The "storming of the Bastille" took place in the second semester and, within minutes of their appearance, I received a phone call from the district that they had reassigned the teacher. I knew this transfer would mean an end to the harm faced by my kids, but the reality of what might happen to others left a hole in my heart.

For the first time in my career, I decided to write letters to every college where the students in this teacher's class had applied. I indicated that because of extenuating circumstances, I was requesting that the admissions committees disregard the first quarter grades in this special class that would appear on their applicant's transcript. I owed it to our students and their very caring and supportive parents to reach out to these universities.

The kids were fortunate in this case to have a good ending thanks to their parents. More importantly, the colleges were willing to disregard the original failing grade from the student transcripts.

There were times, however, when parents did make unreasonable demands on me and my staff about changing grades. I did have to intervene, on occasion, to see if there was any validity in a complaint regarding a teacher's evaluation of a student. Most of the time it was very clear that the youngster did not fulfill the course requirements resulting in a lower rating. There were situations when the grade was truly in question. Our instructors were often agreeable in giving leeway to rethinking the grade in extenuating circumstances. Yet I never changed a grade without the teacher's approval.

I know there are nightmare stories of principals in other schools engaging in this practice, especially to help kids with eligibility for sports teams. Most of the time the teachers were justified, but you just could not underestimate the parents. I found that even when kids came from the most horrendous of family and home situations, there was always someone in the household who realized that something going on in school just didn't seem right and made arrangements to discuss the issues with me.

There were times, however, when our different worlds did come into conflict. I learned to be patient since many of our parents were extremely stressed over the demands being placed on them, especially as single caretakers. Yet this one incident did require me to give a reality check to one individual. This parent was called in for a pre-suspense hearing since her daughter had gotten into a fight with another student. The code of discipline in the city required principals to hold a conference with the parent to go over the charges and consequences associated with the child's behavior prior to the start of the suspension. School regulations mandated that kids who handle conflict by fighting must be punished with an in-home suspension. When the parent was called in to my office, she did not agree with this decision and began to scream at me, accusing me of being insensitive because I was a "rich principal with a fancy car." I was not sure where she got this notion, but I was in the mood for a good laugh. I asked the parent to come with me into the schoolyard where I parked my "fancy car."

We proceeded to move toward my fifteen-year-old, rusty, broken-down Toyota Corolla, which truly surprised and almost frightened the parent. To add salt to the wound I opened the door to my car and slammed it shut with enough force so that a piece of the corroded door could break off. The parent was in shock when I asked her how she liked my "fancy car." She was speechless, but I got a good chuckle. I "truly" enjoyed driving this old jalopy to work especially to a neighborhood where cars were frequently vandalized. Fortunately, this case was isolated, and most often our parents were cooperative and appreciative of the sacrifices made by our staff.

Through the years, our parent advocates did make a positive impact on our school culture. Their service on our leadership teams and advisory councils brought them closer to the teaching staff. They helped foster a new respect for the instructors and administrators, as they became more familiar with schoolwide programs and activities. In several cases, we even arranged for them to volunteer in the guidance office, college office, general office, cafeteria, and hallways. This connection became invaluable to me over time. They earned a great reputation by becoming an asset to the school and very much appreciated as team members.

Chapter 33 – Joys and Regrets

After nine years serving as a principal and a total of twenty-one years of employment at Manhattan Center, working as a teacher and administrator, I began to seriously consider retirement. During those twenty-one years, I witnessed many changes in personnel, student populations, district and citywide leaders, mayors, state curriculum, and standardized exam requirements. The world had changed dramatically in the thirty-plus years since I began my teaching career in 1971. I was feeling quite accomplished in my ability to break down barriers and remove obstacles to teaching and learning throughout my entire run. The most important concept I came to understand was that the "one size fits all" application to education was simply untenable. Although I experienced so many wonderful successes, there were still some unsettled issues with which I just could not seem to make headway.

Of course, my greatest sense of accomplishment came from the increased academic scholarship and student achievement across the board, covering all content areas. I tip my hat to most of my teachers and their dynamic assistant principals for sharing their dedication and passion in raising expectations and standards. The teachers were the ones on the front lines and in the trenches, fighting for improvement every day, taking full responsibility for their outcomes. Once they began working cohesively, they also took on the responsibility of improving their colleagues' results through increased networking, mentoring, and staff development. As this camaraderie increased, the earlier "blame game" attitude decreased. Most instructors bought into the new forms of instruction, and more importantly, they took ownership of the work at hand. We worked together as a true team, and finally stopped defining our culture as "us" and "them."

My successes in getting staff to create more consistent calendars of lessons and standardized subject matter to be taught within each department bore fruit, with improved results being reported across the disciplines. This was no small feat, as I had to battle some of the more obstinate instructors who disagreed with the requirement of having to teach certain state-mandated topics. Some initially disagreed so vehemently that they simply did not want to teach the required material at all. Many teachers felt insulted since they considered themselves to be "professionals," and decisions regarding content should be left to them.

Establishing consensus was one thing, but everyone having individual autonomy by doing something different would totally eliminate accountability and measurement of learning. This notion of teamwork proved to be an asset for me years later. I spent seven years consulting with the principals in the Miami public high schools. I helped them to set up career academies where teams of four teachers worked collaboratively in clusters sharing the same students. The success of one teacher led to the success of all. This feeling of mutual accountability created a new culture in the schools, which became contagious. Soon after, many other teachers wanted to sign on to the career academy initiative. The mission and vision of the schools became a shared responsibility. Today there are over sixty career academies in the Miami schools thanks to dedicated professionals who see the value of working collaboratively.

For many instructors, the disagreement was not with me but with the curriculum board on the state level. Many teachers felt that the content they were mandated to include in their lessons did not conform to their way of thinking. I tried to help them understand that whether or not we agreed with the state was not the issue since the required exams for a diploma were designed to measure student comprehension of the contents of this mandated course of study. Sadly, this problem was the number one issue I decided to take on as a priority when I took charge. This curriculum battle was a very painful experience for me, as I had to confront a number of inflexible staff members. In the end, objections and disagreements were settled, and I was able to move forward with additional structural changes.

Another sense of satisfaction came from my insistence that the youngsters learn how to think critically. During the 1980s with the advent of technology in the classroom, traditional teaching, along with critical thinking skills, died a horrible death, creating a new generation of youngsters with short attention spans and a need for immediate gratification. The days of memorizing facts, only to regurgitate them on tests, without the vaguest understanding of what they were writing, had to end. The notions of cause and effect, drawing conclusions from facts, and using good judgment in decision-making had all been shoved to the side to make room for expediency.

Teachers of English and history often refused to assign writing projects because they had too many papers to correct. After all, many instructors taught 170 students a day, making this task overwhelming. As a result, kids were often unprepared to write essays on the Regents exams in these areas. I was determined to make content more meaningful and useful once again. My standard advice to teachers became, "What do you want the kids to know, and what do you want them to do with the information?" Some Foreign Language teachers were still creating tests with true/false and matching questions. How can you possibly teach conversational and written skills in a second language with these types of exercises? It just would not work! It was an argument I never thought I would win. However, as the departments moved to standardize their teaching and testing practices, these archaic teaching methods went out the window.

My greatest source of satisfaction came from the staff members who were willing to pull out all the stops to increase the success of our total student population. With the increased instructional time provided by block programming in math and science, the extended day, funded by the Children's Aid Society, and, yes, the "living room" in the basement, our staff was able to create miracles. Even though I will graciously take credit for lobbying, negotiating, and hobnobbing with community people who could make things happen with their generous resources, none of the academic successes could have resulted without my dedicated staff.

Perhaps the greatest cause of frustration for me as an administrator was the way in which I was forced to deal with mediocrity in the delivery of instruction. Neither central headquarters nor the district went far enough in raising red flags on the teachers who were continually rated poorly on their evaluations. These teachers were simply being circulated throughout the city's schools, only to create problems in the next school, leaving it to that principal to deal with the issue. It was debilitating and time-consuming. I guess I should not complain since the culture of Manhattan Center seemed to attract more talented people. However, nationwide union protection of unsatisfactory teachers coupled with archaic rules of seniority built into the educational system rarely take the needs or well-being of the students into account. The truth was that it was the kids who paid the price for the ineptitude of these teachers.

The situation is even worse in many schools where administrators are not even aware when they observe poor teaching in the first place. Some things just don't change. I recall attending a staff development conference in Detroit very recently with one thousand administrators who were asked to observe three videotaped lessons and evaluate them with a rating of one to five. We sat with "clickers" and began to score each lesson based on a set of standardized evaluative criteria with the ratings being tabulated and viewed on a big screen. The results were incredibly embarrassing since the range of grades were so far apart in terms of what constitutes "great teaching." In many cases the same lessons that were graded as superlative by some were seen by others as bordering mediocre to unacceptable. You would have concluded that principals from all over the country would have had similar criteria for what should define excellent instruction. I was totally mortified.

However, I did not have to travel too far to know that right in my own backyard the situation regarding standards for teaching varied from place to place. There was one incident that created such angst for one of my students that I was forced to take action.

I inherited a teacher who had been rated unsatisfactory in Queens, in Brooklyn, and yet again in the Bronx. When I called the previous supervisors for a reference they informed me that the teacher was "good" in the classroom but was rated poorly because of his attendance. No one in any evaluative position took his past performance seriously before he was transferred to Manhattan Center. The district personnel offices did not do their homework or take responsibility in vetting this individual either. The teacher was disgruntled and angry and even admitted that perhaps he should have chosen another profession.

One day, a student whom I had taken under my wing over the years because he was challenged came flying into my office, absolutely hysterical. When I finally calmed him down, he informed me that this teacher had threatened to "knock him out." Once I confirmed the validity of his statement, I immediately called the superintendent's office. Without hesitation, I said to him, "It's the teacher or me. Either you remove the instructor or I walk." The teacher was gone in minutes, but the damage to my student was not easily repaired. Why did it have to take such a drastic incident to convince my colleagues that this teacher should have never been allowed to enter another school building?

This attitude toward teacher education must be addressed. I probably will not be around to witness it. There are so many more "war stories" that my fellow principals and I could repeat over and over again, because of the tremendous frustration we had in not being able to move the needle very much over the years regarding this big issue in NYC schools. The emotional and academic damage to kids cannot be measured.

In terms of instruction, I would have liked to see a more project-based approach to instruction and more interdisciplinary curriculum planning. I always felt that so much information was taught in isolation and, if we could only broaden the subject's relevance to other areas of learning, more critical thinking could take place. Research had indicated that the best way for kids to learn was through an interdisciplinary approach that was linked between subject areas. However, most teachers were either too busy or lacked the confidence to design interdisciplinary lessons. Neither did we provide time in their schedule to accomplish this huge task. We did make headway in having guest speakers and teacher visitations cross over from time to time, but this idea never became systemic. Many teachers did volunteer to rewrite a more connected curriculum, which proved successful when teams worked and taught together in a block or parallel teaching module. For me, it still was never enough. The creative juices needed in planning these kinds of lessons were not far-reaching.

In terms of project-based learning, I would have preferred that every course culminate with a project that was created and defended orally by each student. The benefits of such a project were clear. Writing and speaking skills were important indicators of future success, in spite of technological advances. Topics chosen by the students for these projects were relevant to their own lives, thus allowing them the opportunity to retain more content than they would have derived from the traditional lecture format. However, many instructors felt that the time required to schedule project presentations given by each student would be counterproductive to the actual completion of the curriculum. Perhaps in honors or advanced classes where students and teachers were not as concerned with preparing for the Regents exams, research projects would have been included in the course of study. The career academies that I helped to set up in

Miami included courses that culminated with a project that the kids had been working on throughout the semester. Without the mandate of a state exam such as the Regents in New York the teachers had more flexibility with their time to design curriculum.

The more creative teachers at MCSM would incorporate test preparation skills into their everyday teaching plans. Some of our educators taught to the test, meaning that after May 15 the only teaching going on was exam prep for the rest of the semester. Teaching to the test was not a good practice, but staff members often resorted to this strategy because of their obsession with obtaining better test results.

Looking back over thirty years in the business, the debate between those in favor of standardized tests and those who are stifled by them has never been settled. Rarely do we find the balance or the compromise that incorporates excellent "creative" teaching that also includes a reliable method of measuring the mastery of content and learning. We have argued about it for centuries, and we continue to see it as our biggest problem. Educators and parents nationwide are still fighting it out over the "Common Core" curriculum mandate.

One thing for sure, in the absence of testing for minimal essentials in each content area, we will never know what teachers are teaching or what kids are learning. Without this knowledge we end up with zero accountability. My conclusion is twofold. Excellent teaching will always incorporate built-in measures that indicate whether or not kids are comprehending what is being delivered. This information is easy to ascertain by the questions we ask in class. Since these indicators can be administered in many ways, this understanding leads me to my second conclusion of "one size never fits all."

There should never be one way to measure mastery of instruction or learning, especially since we work with kids from all walks of life with a variety of abilities necessitating enrichment and/or remediation.

Perhaps this notion of a "one size fits all" mentality could account for the poor results seen in many schools regarding Bilingual and Special Education. These two areas of instruction, which should not be seen as the same, do share one thing in common. Children in need of services in either situation need a very customized approach to instruction. Aside from the fact that many folks in our country do not believe that we should be offering Bilingual services to our kids because their grandparents came off the boat in the 1900s without getting any help, we decided to offer a program at MCSM for about 150 students. I fought for their rights early on and headed up a task force in the district to make sure the programs were in compliance. Many models of instruction were designed to address different language deficiencies, but I felt that these services were meant to be temporary as a transition into the "mainstream."

Again, since students from many places arrived in this country with different linguistic needs; the "one size fits all" mentality just wouldn't work. Case in point: After careful diagnosis I realized that many of our kids were very familiar with the contents in their courses, but because they could not express themselves in English they became incapable of passing the tests. So if we had a *wiz* in math or science, and we had many, they ended up failing the courses because they couldn't read or write in English or understand the questions even though their skills in the content area were superlative. As a result, I was immediately on the phone with the State Education Department petitioning for the kids to allow them to write the answers to the Regents exams in their native languages, and also to be allowed to use dictionaries that gave straight translations without meanings or explanations of the terminology or concepts.

Not only did the State give me permission to make these accommodations, but they also suggested hiring Bilingual paraprofessionals to assist the students during their classes and during their exams with English language vocabulary. This practice was soon to be incorporated into the district handbook for other schools to follow. As predicted, scholarship for our bilingual youngsters became markedly improved. At the same time that they were learning English, they continued to be competitive with their counterparts by getting good grades, and not falling behind.

For the longest time teachers were willing to write these kids off to failure, blaming their laziness, immigrant status, and bilingual programs for perpetuating their inability to catch up. Once again, we had to dig deep and aim high for these deserving children.

While I truly understand that many schools sadly hold bilingual students hostage for many years, and graduate them without mastery of English, I have to acknowledge that a "one size fits all" approach is unacceptable. I preferred our kids to be fluent in their native language while becoming literate in English at the same time. Fortunately, I recruited competent teachers who were willing to employ models of excellence that worked while taking the kids' best interests into account. Our goal was also to make these kids truly bilingual.

The challenges with Special Education were much more complex since each student's handicapping disability was radically different. My coordinator of these services was an expert on the laws that we were mandated to follow. I fought hard to have him in my school full-time with the agreement that he would write the bible for the district on regulations and models of instruction. We incorporated team teaching approaches, inclusion models, and mainstreaming initiatives wherever possible. The kids were given internships, job shadowing activities, and assignments throughout the school to be active with the entire school population.

Our general education kids were taught to be sensitive and helpful toward all challenged classmates. We all learned that Special Education was not a "place" but a service. We made sure that "the one size fits all" notion just could not work in our school. We refused to follow a mandated set of stringent rules that were meant to be applied to all children. We needed to be flexible, and customize a learning package for each individual kid with a disability.

Case in point: A youngster and his mother insisted that the rigors of an Advanced Placement class could easily be handled. Against the teacher's advice, we placed the student in the class knowing that the challenge would be great considering the youngster's learning disabilities. Since this course was probably one of the most demanding classes we offered, the teacher felt that the kid would not be able to keep up. Well, as predicted, the assignments were not turned in, and the child seemed to be daydreaming during the lessons. When the parent was made aware of the situation, she insisted that we provide a tutor in the class to assist the student since the child had an attention deficit issue but was still absorbing the material. When May came, and the teacher recommended that the kid not sign up for the exam, the parent went ballistic. She continued to insist that her child knew the material well enough to sit for the AP test.

Well, we honored the parent's request, allowing the youngster to take the test, and to our astonishment, the student placed very high. The teacher and I did not know what to make of this finding but were sure to remember this incident for the future. The model we used, thanks to the parent being an advocate for her child, was the proof that one size never, never fits all. Whether it comes from me or the teacher or the parent, when it comes to kids, we need to dig deep and aim high.

As a side note, if I ever have to single out any group of teachers who deserve the greatest commendation, it goes to the folks who provide Special Education services. These educators, by far, have the most difficult and challenging job in the world trying to teach children who face tough odds on a daily basis. I take my hat off to all of them who truly want to do "good" by kids. I thank them for persevering and "aiming high" for all of our youngsters.

Chapter 34 – The Turn of the Century Brings a Life-Changing Decision

The year 2000 came and went without the alarming results of prognosticators who warned of exploding computers, ships without navigational equipment, or the parting of the seas. For us at Manhattan Center, it was business as usual. For me personally, life as an educator put me in a position to truly evaluate the results of our efforts to change the norm in delivering instruction to our students.

My ability to track the changes in academic success over a five- to ten-year period gave me a tremendous amount of satisfaction, as it revealed real and documented growth. My evaluations as a principal continued to be more favorable, as the rate of failure in coursework and on Regents exams dropped significantly, and summer school attendees were kept to a minimum. My reputation throughout the Manhattan high schools was stellar, although I was one of fifty other great leaders. I was often being asked to mentor other supervisors on programming, afterschool initiatives, and establishing protocols for just about anything.

Our school was credited for creating roadmaps for Special Education and English As A Second Language/Bilingual services. With a number of years of experience as a principal under my belt, I was now considered to be a "veteran," and so I was always flattered when asked to help fellow administrators. My superintendent seemed to be pleased with the way I was running my school plant. Yet, my own continued obsession with the data created a daily sense of unease. I always felt so responsible in handling the monies provided by GE, Mt. Sinai, and the Children's Aid Society, striving to make every penny produce two cents' worth of results.

My efforts to engage in "business as usual" were, however, interrupted by the worst domestic terrorist attack ever to be perpetrated on our city.

On September 11, 2001, two commercial airplanes were hijacked in the air by terrorists and flown into the two buildings that were known as the World Trade Center. For the schools in the immediate vicinity of the explosions, evacuations of the teachers and staff put them in grave danger, as toxic gasses and falling debris were everywhere. The entire city was in chaos. Parents couldn't locate their children. Children couldn't locate their parents. Family members were desperate to ascertain the whereabouts of their loved ones. The losses incurred by our communities were unprecedented. The fear and panic experienced by every student and teacher were palpable. Everyone knew of someone who had experienced a loss. MCSM was designated as a Command Center, which put us in the center of it all.

Crisis intervention teams were immediately dispatched. The entire school system was paralyzed. Our students lost parents in the attack. I lost alumni who had taken jobs at the location of the explosions. It was devastating. Yet, I took great pride in the actions of my fellow teachers, administrators, and support personnel who stepped up to the plate on the most challenging day in our country's domestic history. Our security team and local police force continued to perform heroic acts. From that day forward, our lives would be categorized as "before 9/11" and "after 9/11." The schools and the world around us would never be the same.

Certainly, in terms of my own leadership, I was put to the test once again. The vision of the chaos in the building would linger in my mind forever. I had to provide emotional support and direction to the staff and children in all three of my schools. I remember hearing screaming in the halls mostly from the adults. Many of the male teachers were visibly crying. It was deafening. The fear came more from not knowing what was going to come next since shortly after the Twin Tower disaster several other planes were reported to have crashed.

For the kids the biggest issue was transportation as we were given instructions to dismiss them so that they could be with their families. Since many of the buses and subways were being halted the students were not sure how they were going to get home. It was not until late into the evening that we finally rerouted all the children with alternate means of travel. Throughout the day the sounds of sirens, fire trucks, and ambulances made us all feel even more on edge.

If you looked out the window you could see thick black smoke covering the sky even though we were nine miles away from the explosion. We ushered the students into the auditorium, gyms, cafeteria, and playgrounds to be able to provide very creative crisis intervention. As usual, most of the staff stood tall and made us proud. My own personal grief and shock had to be put aside as students, parents, and the entire community looked to us for answers and prayers.

Consolation and guidance were easy for us since we had weathered other storms, but answers or explanations for this senseless tragedy were nowhere to be found. We had to deal with crisis management on a daily basis and hope that time would be a healer. Sadly, for some who dealt with real personal losses, the struggle was even greater. My dear friend and colleague who was an administrator of a school right under the smoke of the buildings led her kids out of harm's way. As she looked up to the sky, she knew that a family member had perished in the explosion.

After several months, we began to normalize our school operations, though "normal" was far from what we would ever return to see. We had to create evacuation plans, parental communications plans, and revised fire drill plans. Security was stepped up and taken more seriously than ever. Rumors of copycat activities were everywhere. We were on edge. Then, several foolish kids engaged in prank calls, insisting on several occasions that there were bombs in the building. These acts posed a real problem, in that I had to evacuate the school each time these calls came in. It became debilitating. None of the calls were real, but I couldn't take a chance.

Periodically, kids were pulling the fire alarms so we could abandon classes. Our security personnel had to spray the alarm handles with blue invisible ink in order to catch the culprits. Fortunately, these mischievous youngsters were caught, and the kids came to understand that these activities were considered criminal and came with serious consequences. The prank calls soon abated, and we returned to the job of preparing the kids for graduation and an exciting college career. Each day became easier as we approached the winter months.

In 2002, I received an unexpected call from my boss. His voice was cheerful and positive, so I was relieved that there didn't seem to be a problem. Surprisingly, he called to ask if I would consider applying to become his deputy. I was stunned by the offer and, though I'm never at a loss for words, I was truly in shock. I replied that I would take his offer into consideration and would get back to him quickly.

When I hung up, I was actually shaking like a leaf. Although I was flattered by his offer, I was not an administrative office kind of person. I loved being surrounded by my kids. I couldn't even consider giving up my morning meetings with my students, chasing children down the hallways, making classroom presentations, teaching leadership, and attending award ceremonies. The thought of giving up the opportunity to help teachers be all they could be and observing them perform miracles in the classroom with our inner-city kids wasn't sitting well with me. My decision soon became a moot point but was also fueled by another issue circulating throughout the city.

A rumor was rumbling around the schools that Mayor Bloomberg and the chancellor were strongly considering consolidating the entire city school system of over one million kids and close to two thousand schools. I had heard that thirty-two school district offices serving elementary and middle school students and five borough-wide high school offices would be dissolved. Superintendents would be reassigned and, for the first time since the late 1960s, the decentralized schools and local school boards would be collapsed. Districts would become "regions." Offices would be turned into classrooms, and millions of dollars would be saved with the elimination of hundreds of employees.

Since the school system was under the auspices of the mayor, the truth was in the rumor. Since becoming the mayor of New York City, Bloomberg and the chancellor ran the school system in a business-like manner. I totally agreed with the move to eliminate the culture of corruption and mismanagement in the decentralized school districts. However, the high school borough offices served an extremely important purpose. Experts on many issues had a great track record of providing multiple levels of support and expertise to the principals, assistant principals, teachers, and parents. Their many years of experience gave credibility to their purpose. Perhaps a bit of cost-saving would have been in order, but the elimination of this important resource for all who took advantage of it would predictably be devastating.

Given the possibility that the role of superintendents would be nonexistent, I advised my boss that I would not be taking him up on his offer for a number of reasons. I did not want to elaborate on this "rumor" since the possibility of the upcoming changes to the system might jeopardize his own future. I included the thought that, perhaps, this might be the optimum time for me to consider retirement. It certainly wouldn't be fair to accept the job as his deputy, only to leave within a year or two. I indicated that if I couldn't give him a minimum of five years, I couldn't really be an asset. He appreciated my honesty, was deeply disappointed, but respected my decision. The seed to consider retirement was planted that day.

I didn't want to be impulsive and make such a life-changing decision prematurely, especially because so many rumors were flying around regarding systemwide changes to the Department of Education. The reorganization plan would make a tremendous impact on teachers, on students, and on administrators. I was not clear about what the end result might look like for the city. Further, I had to think long and hard about leaving my dream job, one for which I had worked my entire career. I know, it's difficult to understand how working in a tough, poverty-ridden, crime-stricken neighborhood and checking into a roach-infested mousetrap of an office could be considered a dream job. Yet, I loved these kids with all my heart.

Each morning as I greeted them one by one upon entering the cafeteria, the difficulties of my working conditions faded away. This place was, indeed, my home away from home. In fact, I spent more time at school than I actually did at home. I had created a mutual respect for the community residents, storekeepers, the people of faith from the church across the street, the 25th Police Precinct, and, of course, my very supportive and dedicated staff.

On the other hand, I was always told that one should leave the party when the celebrations and festivities were burning bright, the noise was loud, and the excitement high. The advice always included the message of not waiting to leave when the flame was beginning to flicker, when the cheering crowd was thinning out, or when the food was getting cold. Translated into educational parlance, one should consider retiring when the school is operating at its peak. Besides, I did not want to wait for the day when the kids might say that this guy is getting old and confused and needs to go home.

My results were as good as they could get, although I always reminded myself that I could dig deeper. The culture of the school and the positive attributes of how we conducted business—from delivery of instructional excellence to security and classroom management; from outstanding attendance and graduation numbers to community involvement—finally became systemic. I knew that if I retired, I would be leaving the place, with all of its million pieces, in great shape. How the next leader would adopt my message or change the establishment would not be known to me. I knew for a very long time that no one was indispensable, but at least I knew that I would pass the torch fully lit. Above all, I was content with our willingness and ability as a staff to dig deep and aim high.

Chapter 35 – A Fairy Tale Ending

It was early fall 2003, and I was inching closer to that all-important decision of packing it in by the end of August 2004, just before the start of the school year.

No one other than my wife knew of my intentions, although my conversations with the superintendent and rumors moving through the school building sent out a message that sooner or later my retirement announcement would be made. My wife was nervous and concerned about my retirement, as sharing me with the New York City Department of Education for so many years had become a way of life. Aside from several short getaways, we both felt as though we hadn't seen each other for over twenty years when I became an administrator. Leaving home early in the morning and not returning home until late at night most days left little time for family. Weekend school visits just exacerbated the situation. Time together was certainly on my wish list, but I had to create an exit plan. Part of that plan was to leave the next administrator with a neatly wrapped package of academic scholarship. This final year of my career at MCSM had to be the best one yet.

During the summer of 2003, I sat for my end-of-year evaluation with the superintendent. As usual, I submitted my thick book of documentation, including graphs and charts full of statistics, extrapolated and disaggregated in multiple ways to produce a complete picture of our accomplishments. He was totally pleased with the outcomes. Yet, he had one particular question for me, which had come up in previous evaluations. He was still wondering how I was physically able to interview every senior twice, evaluate their transcripts, and visit every senior classroom periodically during the year. In addition, he wanted to know why I was the one doing these visits and not the guidance counselors, college advisors, or senior grade advisors. It was not that he doubted my word. It was simply that no one had ever mentioned doing this before.

I explained that the kids were the most important part of my successes. Being close to the children reconfirmed why I went into this business in the first place. I further responded that although the counselors and advisors were generally on top of their game and did make many visits to classrooms, the number of kids in their caseloads was very large. I always feared that some of the seniors would fall through the cracks. So, okay, maybe I was a control freak, but over the years too many students had missed graduation because they were missing one credit or one course. None of the counselors were at fault, but a second pair of eyes couldn't hurt.

We never knew what to anticipate. Financial aid and scholarship money were also at stake. For the sake of the students and their parents, I was trying to avoid this embarrassment. I needed to send out a warning prior to their arrival at the point of no return. My boss indicated that with a senior class of over four hundred students, this oversight was unavoidable, but remained in awe of my desire, or perhaps my obsession, with the implementation of such a time-consuming, exhausting guidance effort.

I have to say that my counselors and grade advisors were the best you could find and did save lives in many cases when the kids were in crisis. The truth was really that I absolutely loved to visit the students in their classes, see their facial expressions when I made old-fashioned and out-of-date comments, and watch their eyes light up when we spoke of college, the prom, and graduation. This connection always brought us closer. I guess it was part of my paternal instinct.

The superintendent and I parted ways with a tremendous amount of mutual respect. This guy was close to seven feet tall and spoke with the most incredible vocabulary. After every meeting I would go home and look up the definitions of his words without admitting to anyone my ignorance. For me, this leader was literally a giant and truly wanted me to be the best I could be. In spite of his size he left with tears in his eyes.

As it turned out, the mayor's reorganization plan was implemented in the fall of 2003. All of the superintendents were either reassigned or encouraged to leave. Their positions were dissolved and many principals remaining were fearful of what additional changes might come their way with a negative impact. Several of my very accomplished and most competent superintendents did leave to take on jobs in other places. So many dedicated professionals were forced to vacate their offices and renounce their titles. The resource people and staff developers who provided daily support for all things educational in the life of a high school were gone.

The coming year would be absolute torture for many administrators who found their "go to" person dismissed without replacement. There wasn't even a person who could sign off on important documents that required a district employee's signature. Everyone was gone. We were on our own. I do remember how early on in my career when I worked in the middle school I criticized the corruption and cronyism of the decentralized school boards. Yet, now they were throwing out the baby with the bathwater. Tremendous pockets of talent and experience were now all gone, leaving a training ground for replication of best practices to a thing of the past.

It pained me to see that City Hall looked at education as a business and was willing to dismiss dedicated leaders with incredible track records. This move was a big part of the master plan. It was always felt that many of us educators used antiquated practices to run our schools and were responsible for the poor results in the city. While I agreed that there was a good amount of bloat in this educational bureaucracy that needed to be addressed, filling the empty spaces with very young and inexperienced folks from private industry who knew nothing about teaching or learning made absolutely no sense.

With twenty-one years of high school administrative experience under my belt, it was deeply insulting to have to take direction from someone in an unrelated industry. Perhaps their success in the private sector could have served to inform the schools where appropriate, but to put them in charge of schools without ever having taught, or without any experience in education, struck me as being very damaging.

Case in point: A twenty-five-year-old appointee paid an unexpected visit to my school, snooping around every nook and cranny, observing classes, and scrutinizing our profile. I did not know who he was, other than being told he was from the DOE. His comment to me at the end of his visit was simply that I needed to better decorate my lobby. He was gone, but the next day I received a follow-up call from the department advising me as well to "better decorate my lobby." I think this call might have been a sign.

Children are not data points that can be fed into a computer with the hope that the result will be consistent. There are so many elements that go into the education of inner-city kids; so many extenuating factors that play into their behavior, their learning capacity, their emotional well-being. They don't function like people in a business. I am sure that there were exceptions, and that a number of young, inexperienced people from other industries did become successful principals. However, in general, what could be said about working your way up, learning the trade, and reflecting upon years of experience if we assign folks without the credentials?

Many of my colleagues told me that I would know when it would be the right time to retire. This reorganization plan was the catalyst for my departure.

The formal announcement to my staff took place at a teachers' recognition ceremony in March 2004. I wanted everyone to be in a festive mood when I gave them the news. At 3:00 it is difficult to be festive after a long and arduous day. However, I knew that when you feed people, they are more receptive. When the words of my departure finally rolled off my tongue, the room broke into applause. Were they actually happy to see me go? Even the few folks who never joined my bandwagon and gave me so much grief congratulated me and expressed the feeling that I deserved some peace and quiet after so many years of service.

One by one, the teachers came up to me with mixed emotions, glad for me but fearful of who might replace me. I spent the next several months calming everyone down, assuring them that I was grooming someone who would be a positive for MCSM. Some staff even asked who would host the annual holiday party, something my wife and I had done for the past ten years. This yearly event was indeed a joyous occasion to which everyone in the building, including the security staff, custodial crew, and cafeteria workers, were invited.

Little by little, the students began hearing about my impending retirement. Some came into my office begging me to stay. The juniors, especially, were disappointed that I wouldn't be part of their lives for the entire four years of their high school experience. I did promise to attend the next several graduations to at least give each grade with whom I worked a proper send-off. Besides, the daughter of my former student Connie was now a student in the school, and I owed it to my "newly adopted grandchild" Maisha that I would attend her graduation and hand her a diploma. I did keep my promise. The edition of the student newspaper that was issued following my retirement announcement had the heading, "Askinazi Gives up the Helm." I was flattered. This was for real.

There were numerous celebrations to follow and a retirement party for three hundred guests in an event space overlooking the Hudson River and the New York skyline. I never felt deserving of such an elaborate show of recognition, but my staff was very insistent. My colleagues, community leaders, and folks from private industry representing the numerous collaboratives that our students enjoyed were all present. The most emotional part of the evening came when an alumnus, who flew out from the West Coast to honor me, spoke of my influence on her life. She was now a university professor who had written a book, and during her speech she highlighted my efforts to encourage her to stay in school and make a successful life for herself.

There were tributes, both spoken and sung, from my staff. My thirty-minute speech was a testament to my faculty, who persevered and fought so hard to create a successful environment for our kids, against all odds. It was also a testament to the students who felt they needed to attend to show their appreciation for everything they received from our staff. After all, they were conditioned from birth to limit their expectations for success. At MCSM, they were always pushed to pick themselves up when they fell down. We instilled in them the belief that failure was not an option. Music and speeches lasted beyond midnight on a weekday, with work following the next morning. It was a night to remember.

I wasn't done yet! The month of June was always the most tumultuous. For nineteen years, I had conducted graduation ceremonies. This year, although it would be my last, would be an emotional celebration of the achievements of my kids. The many rehearsals scheduled in preparation for commencement were designed to emphasize my desire to make this day a very prestigious event with a classy atmosphere. We would not tolerate catcalls, balloons, or any form of unruly behavior as seen with many schools. The students, parents, and staff deserved the utmost respect for accomplishing the unimaginable.

This great day finally came. I conducted the graduation ceremony in English and Spanish, creating an inclusive atmosphere. However, for the first time in all the years I had emceed the celebrations, something unusual occurred. Toward the end of the ceremony, after all the graduates had accepted their diplomas and I was ending my speech, a young lady from the audience took the steps to the stage and grabbed the microphone from my hand. I was initially stunned and confused, but soon understood what was happening. She proceeded to identify herself as a former graduate and announced my retirement to the audience. Everyone was asked to stand at their seats as two students from each of the MCSM graduating classes, beginning in 1986, marched down the aisle in a procession, walked on the stage, and gave me a huge hug. I was absolutely shocked and, for the second time in my career, I was speechless. I could not control my emotions and broke down into tears. I couldn't stop the audience from cheering. Next, the school choir and band began playing songs of appreciation, and several faculty members sang tributes.

Finally, after all calmed down, I made the final decree of my career to the graduates. "By the power vested in me...I now declare you graduates of Manhattan Center High School for Science and Mathematics." As I regained my composure, I walked out the front doors after graduation, only to find hundreds of parents waiting outside to offer their own words of thanks and appreciation, along with more hugs. It was an unforgettable day, one that has been stored in the archives of special days of my life.

My job responsibilities were still not over, as I had to return to the building to open the doors to the summer school session once more. I guess it was an additional sign that it was time for me to retire when the summer proved to be one of the hottest on record. Without air conditioning, it was especially difficult for the kids, as their discomfort impacted on their absorption of the subject matter. With each passing day, I was one day closer to retirement.

On the last day of my tenure as principal of MCSM, I said my final goodbyes. Yet, I needed to ask a favor of one of my colleagues. I was too emotional to exit the building on my own, so I asked him to escort me to my car. I refused to look back. I didn't want to see the school behind me after having it front and center for so many years. I knew I was giving up an incredible gift that I would never be able to get back. We walked to my car. I got in, cried for half an hour, and finally left the campus, heading home for the very last time. This was my fairy tale ending.

Epilogue

Every teacher, every administrator, and every educator has a different takeaway when exiting the system after many years of service. Some look at their departure with a "been there, done that" reaction. Others congratulate themselves for surviving and being able to collect a decent pension. Hopefully, however, many others will look back over their career with a greater sense of accomplishment.

I am proud to say that I still get very passionate and energized about my life in this profession.

I experienced the worst of times and the best of times during my tenure in the public schools. My days in middle school and my time in high school were dramatically different in terms of what I encountered regarding culture, teaching, learning, and student growth.

Clearly, there were many common denominators that could be found throughout all levels of public education, and which could also be applicable to inner-city schools in other parts of the country. Discussions on how to best teach kids, especially in very large bureaucratic systems, will always be ongoing.

The union politics described in my chapters may have given the false impression that I was anti-union. Certainly, there is a need to have strong unions in any industry to serve as a balance of power to those in government who would prefer to weaken an organization that strives for better treatment and protections for their constituents. Specifically, in education, unions can protect their members when faced with dictatorial or narrow-minded supervisors or when personal or political pressures substitute for just cause. I did hear through the "grapevine" that there were administrators who were abusive and made some poor decisions. There will always be errors in judgment from both sides, and the lines between management and union will always be drawn.

I am pleased when I observe and read about schools nationwide with union-endorsed staff development programs and workshops that have been created to raise the level of professionalism within its ranks. These offerings at our school always made me feel like we were finally moving away from "us and them." I also know that the fringe benefits negotiated by the unions, whether they be in salaries, healthcare, or retirement safety nets, often make the difference between thriving or merely surviving. Protecting their members from targeted layoffs, budget cuts, unacceptable transfers, or toxic work environments is well documented.

However, the moment the union politics in our schools overlook the well-being of the children by accepting mediocrity, we end up taking kids out of the equation. In exchange for protecting the members at all costs, the value of the union is compromised. The protection of unsatisfactory, even dangerous employees in the schools continues to be my greatest source of dissatisfaction with the entire educational bureaucracy. There has to be a better and more expedient process to extricate an educator, teacher, or administrator who proves over and over again to be incapable of doing the job. At least we need to explore more effective strategies to better prepare our teachers and offer them more help on the job to avoid an impasse.

The clock is always ticking for kids, and we cannot make up for the loss of instruction while the teacher is working semester after semester trying to figure it out. To expect an administrator to spend months, even years, defending his or her actions against an unsatisfactory teacher at all these hearings is unreasonable. Taking all this time away from other important duties of the job at hand is a loss to everyone. It should not take years to resolve a dispute. Our kids deserve better. The costs of these litigations, both in time and money, could easily pay for additional resources for students and teachers. We must change our priorities when evaluating teacher competency.

At the same time, we must up our game as to how we educate the prospective educators at the university level. The age-old criticism, which I myself experienced while in college, of professors who have never taught a day in their lives, pretending to be able to provide realistic, accurate guidance about teaching in an inner city is preposterous! I would suggest that teacher preparation departments partner with local school districts to provide internships, apprenticeships, and field work as a means to better expose future teaching candidates for the job they will encounter. This partnership should be initiated with the very first education course elected. This process would eliminate those students (future teachers) who feel they could not handle the stressors early on. Further, districts would be recruiting personnel with a true understanding of what to expect based on observation, with actual teaching experience under their belts. What better way to strengthen the pool of educators?

On the school level, support can come in many forms. More teachers should be encouraged to take on education interns, open their classrooms as models to others who might need new creative sources, and teach them to buy into anticipatory teaching in their lesson planning. This practice is critical for an educator because it allows the teacher to "anticipate" the path they plan in taking to reach the required end or goal. Many folks plan their lessons without questioning where they want their kids to be at the end of the day. Good lesson planning is like conducting a dress rehearsal. After a while, we tend to get lazy and too laid-back, minimizing the importance of having workable and flexible written plans. Without a plan, what mechanisms do we have to make sure kids are being held accountable for their learning?

Finally, teachers should be respected for their role in society, to mold the next generation. In New York City, teachers are required to hold New York State Certification and are required to complete a master's degree program before entering a classroom. All of this preparation requires a significant financial outlay. Yet, teachers nationwide often wait years between contract ratifications, depriving educators of salaries that keep up with inflation. Great strides have been made in many places, while other districts are still struggling.

In addition, working conditions in the deteriorating school buildings continue to be dramatically inferior to those of their suburban counterparts even in the same state. Sadly, members of the teaching profession throughout the country have the same issue and are called upon to tolerate working in this environment.

Today, teaching involves educating, parenting, engaging in social work, employing psychology, and giving all of your soul. Life becomes a juggling act in an attempt to meet the demands of the students, parents, administrators, school districts, city leaders, and an often unappreciative public. The oft-repeated comment that educators have summer and holiday vacations and do not deserve better does not take into account the added burdens they are asked to carry.

This country needs to do more to ensure that our kids will be all they can be, for their sake and for ours. We love them, and they are our future. We should bless our hardworking teachers! They deserve all that we can do for them.

Acknowledgments

Many thanks to the following people without whom I could not have reached my career goals:

My predecessors at Manhattan Center who were great principals, and who demonstrated incredible leadership

The entire faculty at Manhattan Center for their dedication to the students

The community-based organizations in East Harlem that provided our children with valuable resources

The mentors and volunteers from our public/private partnerships for the generosity of time and resources extended to Manhattan Center students and faculty

The 25th Police Precinct in Manhattan for protecting our entire school community

The Manhattan High School District Office for their very professional support

School District Four for their creation and support of Manhattan Center

The Department of Education and the High School Division in NYC for their endorsement of my official appointment as principal of Manhattan Center for Science and Mathematics

My colleagues at the middle school where I taught in my early years for their support in helping me to be a strong role model

The children and parents in NYC who put their trust in me and in my team members

As always, my loving family who shared me with the East Harlem Community for many years

CPSIA information can be obtained
at www.ICGtesting.com
Printed in the USA
LVHW052031210221
679514LV00003B/200